Cultural China

The Mighty Yangtze

China's Life-giving River

By the Creators of CCTV's
Rediscovering the Yangtze River

Better Link Press

This book is edited and designed by the Editorial Committee of *Cultural China* series

Managing Directors: Wang Youbu, Xu Naiqing
Editorial Director: Wu Ying
Editors: Yang Xinci, Deborah Wallace
Editorial Assistant: Li Mengyao

Text and Photos by the Creators of CCTV's *Rediscovering the Yangtze River*
Translation by Wu Xiaozhen

Interior and Cover Design: Yuan Yinchang, Li Jing, Xia Wei

ISBN: 978-1-60220-307-5

Address any comments about *The Mighty Yangtze: China's Life-giving River* to:

Better Link Press
99 Park Ave
New York, NY 10016
USA
or
Shanghai Press and Publishing Development Company
F 7 Donghu Road, Shanghai, China (200031)
Email: comments_betterlinkpress@hotmail.com

Computer typeset by Yuan Yinchang Design Studio, Shanghai
Printed in China by Shanghai Donnelley Printing Co. Ltd.

1 2 3 4 5 6 7 8 9 10

CONTENTS

Foreword

For years the Yangtze River has been like a mother, winding her way; always faithfully providing but displaying drastically different moods to her children. Despite its capriciousness there have always been infinite promises of life. Like many other great rivers in the world known as cradles of civilization, the Yangtze River created fertile soil as it carried and re-arranged the silt from floods and the sand from its bed. Since the dawn of civilization, human life has been thriving along its banks.

The Yangtze River emanates from the south-western side of the snow-draped Gela Dandong Peak, the highest peak in the Tanggula Range. From its birth in Qinghai prefecture at the border of Tibet Autonomous region, it flows eastward across the mid-to-south section of the Chinese mainland. Some 6,380 kilometers in length, it comes in a proud third place after the Amazon in South America and the Nile in Africa.

The snow-draped Gela Dandong Peak

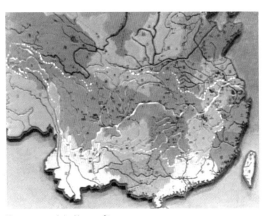

The streams of the Yangtze River

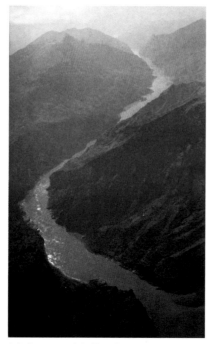

A bird's eye view of the Three Gorges

The mainstream of the Yangtze River traverses ten provinces, municipalities and autonomous regions—Qinghai, Tibet, Sichuan, Yunnan, Hubei, Hunan, Jiangxi, Anhui, Jiangsu and Shanghai—before emptying into the East China Sea.

Over 700 rivers and streams in Gansu, Shaanxi, Henan, Guizhou, Guangxi and Zhejiang join with the Yangtze along the way, paying tribute with their waters and depositions as if greeting their mother.

The Yangtze River Basin drains over an area of 1.8 million square meters, one fifth of China's total land area and 2.5 times the area of the Yellow River Basin.

Since ancient times the Yangtze River has been given many names. It was simply the "River" at the very beginning; then it became known as the "Great River" or the "Yangtze River." Today the commonly acknowledged terms are assigned as follows: it is Tuotuo River from the source to the Chumar River estuary; Tongtian River between the Chumar River estuary and the Batang River estuary at Yushu; Jinsha River between the Batang River estuary and Yibin, Sichuan Province; and the Yangtze River from Yibin until it reaches the sea.

The Boyang Lake

The mainstream of the Yangtze River is divided into upper, middle and lower reaches. The upper reaches extend from the source all the way to Yichang, Hubei Province; the middle reaches stretch from there to Hukou, Jiangxi Province; and the lower reaches lie between Hukou and the sea to the

Satellite remote sensing picture of the Yangtze River

east of Chongming Island. Among the many tributaries of the Yangtze River, are seven major contributors, each with an annual water flow greater than that of the Yellow River. These highly respected tributaries are the Min, Jialing, Wu, Yuan, Xiang, Han, and the Gan Rivers.

The Yangtze River also strings its way to three out of the four largest freshwater lakes in China—Dongting Lake, Boyang Lake and Tai Lake—looking like a vine strung with fruits, forming a huge water system.

The Yangtze River Basin is blessed with fertile soil, plentiful rainfall and mild weather.

With rich mineral resources, abundant products and convenient transportation, the Yangtze River Basin is home to many medium-to-large industrial cities. Together with the Yellow River, it is the cradle of the splendid Chinese civilization, nurturing generation after generation. Like a faithful mother, it goes on contributing to the prosperity of this land.

The Yangtze River Valley, shown within the Map of China. Provided by
China Map Press.

Map of the Yangtze River Valley

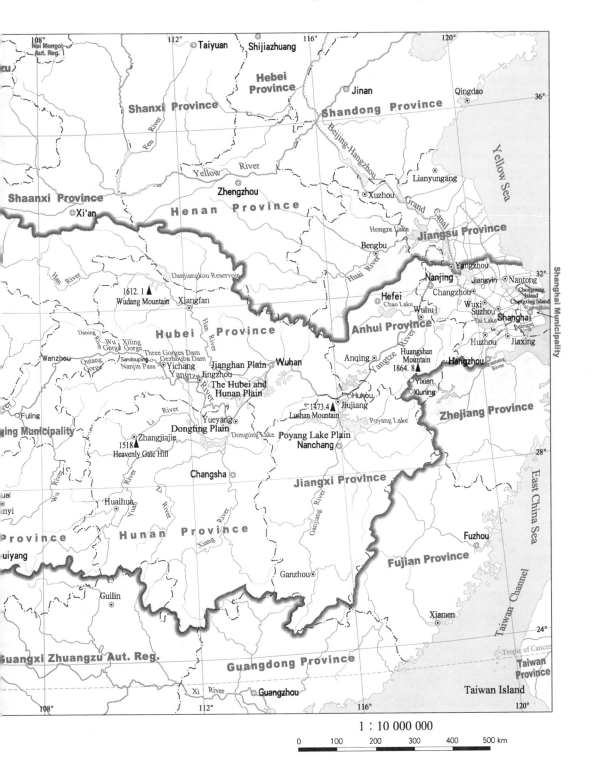

1 : 10 000 000

0   100   200   300   400   500 km

Chapter One
The River Source Revisited

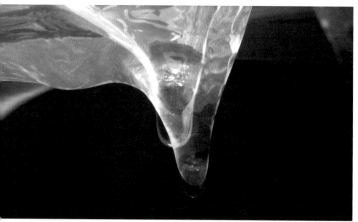

One drop of water from the source of the Yangtze River

Gela Dandong: 91'07"°E, 33'29"°N.

A drop of water emanates from the glaciers of Gela Dandong, in the snowy Qinghai-Tibet Plateau. We will watch this drop of water as it trickles down, starting out on its long journey. Its destination and contribution will vary from its brothers, but each drop has its part to play in the stories that form along the great 6,380-kilometer long Yangtze River.

The story of the Yangtze begins with a mystery. Inquisitive Chinese had been searching up and down the expanses of the Yangtze River on and off for at least 2,000 years but could not definitively confirm its source. It was not until about 300 years ago that people reached the Qinghai-Tibet Plateau searching for what is known as the source area. At that time, they saw a cobweb of creeks stretching towards the horizon, but they still had no idea where the real source was. Treacherous elements and high peaks cloaked over the mystery until 1976, when the first Chinese scientific exploration team entered the Yangtze River source area.

On August 25, 1976, after a 51-day trek through the ice and snow, an exploration team of 28 determined experts located the actual source of the Yangtze River. The mysterious origin of a world-class river was finally known.

On January 13, 1978, China announced to the world: "The Yangtze River originates from Tuotuo River to the southwest of the snowy Gela Dandong,

Glaciers and snowy mountains at the source of the Yangtze River

the highest peak in the Tanggula Range. The total length of the Yangtze River should be 6,380 kilometers—500 kilometers longer than previously recorded."

A month later, the Associate Press reported: "The Yangtze River in China has replaced the Mississippi as the third longest river in the world."

The small Tanggula Mountain Pass: 5,100 Meters above sea level.

The sun has risen and set in the same way for tens of millions of years here. The Garqu Qiangtang, a plateau basin covering an area of 400 square kilometers, is sheltered by the Kunlun Range to its north and the Tanggula Range to its south. There is a river here known as the Garqu River, named after its birthplace, the Garqu Qiangtang. It is here that we take up our journey.

Melted snow at the river source forms the gentle Garqu River that lies across our path, the first river to do so upon our entry into the river source area. At this moment its gentle waves awaken our sense of anticipation.

The silent glaciers thaw in the warm sun, making the river far more threatening than expected in the serene plateau. Its sub-zero water nips, and its maximum depth stands at only 4 meters; but with a force flowing at a powerful 2 meters per second, it is strong enough to carry away a robust yak, venturing one step too close to

The Garqu Qiangtang plateau basin

The rhodiola

the bank.

The weather in the river source area changes "as quickly as the expression on a child's face" it is said. It is not surprising for sleet to descend on the Garqu Qiangtang in August. On this plateau over 5,000 meters above sea level, we encountered danger when crossing the river during the day and endured a snowstorm by night. The same blankets of snow are poetic on the plains, but become a threatening menace, suffocating any huddled traveller if the snow piles too high outside their tent.

Overnight the snowstorm came and went. The sun rose as usual and wild flowers were roused back to life in the morning breeze of Gaerqu. August is the best month at Qiangtang, when flowers and grasses thrive and compete

The plants at the source of the Yangtze River: (from above left to below right) Meconopsis horridula, Pedicularis, Umellate Rockjasmine, Oxytropis falcata Bunge, Buttercup and Carex moorcroftii

Gela Dandong is known as "the Father Mountain of China".

for attention, a month known for the richest color scheme and the gentlest temperament. Yet gentleness reigns here for only few months. During the rest of the year, Qiangtang is an awe-inspiring kingdom where all is white.

Flowers and grasses on the plateau provide us with a good example of "survival of the fittest"; adapting well to their unforgiving environment by keeping small leaves and short stalks and a layer of fluff to protect themselves from the cold and big blossoms to soak in the sun and attract passing winds or insects to help them propagate.

"Qiangtang" in Tibetan means a boggy flat, but the icy, snowy Garqu Qiangtang is hard, frozen earth for most of the year. When flowers come out triumphantly in the fine season, beware that the worst is not over—the melting snow transforms hard land into a bog that might trap you at any moment.

These flowers should delight in their triumph over the Qinghai-Tibet Plateau they call home; they propagate some 5,000 meters above sea level and thrive better than men do. At that height, oxygen levels are only half of those in low-lying areas; with these extreme conditions, it has earned its reputation as the Third Pole of the world.

A snow lotus

The Tanggula Range marks a formidable presence under the clear sky with over 20 snow-draped peaks towering more than 6,000 meters above sea level, extending over 50 kilometers north to south, and over 20 kilometers east to west.

The 6,600-meter tall Gela Dandong stands out proudly in the Tanggula Range. Gela Dandong in Tibetan means "a tall, pointed peak", and its towering figure has earned it the title of "the Father Mountain of China". Above the 5,800-meter snow line of this father, the 70-odd modern glaciers there safeguard the great mother river's mysterious source; the huge reservoir pumps a continuous flow of water into the Yangtze River, preparing her for her long journey.

The ten-odd-kilometer-long Gangjiaquba glacier, the largest among more than 70 modern glaciers of Gela Dandong, is the source of the Garqu River. Some people compare those glaciers to children of Gela Dandong that have grown in their own ways.

Water drips continuously from the melting glaciers. Drips become drops, drops become trickles, and trickles become rapids that break out of the confines of the great glaciers and break the sacred silence of billions of years.

The lines on the rocks at the foot of the snowy peak, impressions left by the flows of water and movements of the glaciers over tens of billions of years' time, show what a powerful force

The mottled moraines

The Jianggendiru Glacier

the glaciers really are.

Ancient water newly emerged out of the glaciers is by no means clear. It is clear only after repeated filtration through pebbly shoals. Those mottled moraines record the movements of earth crust and glaciers since ancient times. Each small piece of them mirrors the spectacular vastness of glaciers. Time brings immense changes to the world; a world through which the Yangtze River is always flowing.

Thawing water from the more than 70 glaciers becomes the Yangtze River source. According to statistics, Gela Dandong glaciers contain fresh water resources equal to two years' flow of the Yellow River. In addition, 26 of these so-called "children" of Gela Dandong are still growing and extending, ensuring the Yangtze River source against depletion.

Right below the snow line snow lotuses brave the cracks among rocks. One of the few plants growing at the highest altitude on earth, the snow lotus is crowned king of all plateau flowers.

We are closing in on that first drop of water. It is there in a glacier of the Jianggendiru Peak, to the southwest of Gela Dandong. If we took a bird's eye view, we would see two jagged modern glaciers embracing the Jianggendiru Peak from the southern and northern sides. The exploration team 30 years ago identified the Tuotuo River as the first section of the Yangtze River because "its source is the furthest inland and its course, the straightest". It is at Jianggendiru that the Tuotuo River forms.

After scientific measurement, the 12.8-kilometer-long, Jianggendiru Glacier to the south was identified as the authentic source of the Yangtze River. Standing at 5,800 meters, the glacier is the highest source for the third longest

The snowy mountains in the source of the Yangtze River

Tuotuo River forms a braided water system.

of the world's great rivers.

Once out of Gela Dandong, the Tuotuo River plays along its way, forming what is known in geology as a braided water system. If we look at it from a distance, we could pick out two other rivers out of the crowded water system that run parallel to it on the north and south, respectively. The Tuotuo River, the Dangqu River and the Chumar River all contribute to the first section of the Yangtze River.

The Tuotuo River, 642.1 kilometers in length.

The 6,380-meter Yangtze River starts with the Tuotuo River, making it the only glacier-born river in the world.

The Dangqu River, 641.1 kilometers in length.

The Dangqu River, the southern source of the Yangtze River, originates from the east side of the Tanggula Range. Dangqu in Tibetan means "a swampland". The Dangqu flows out through gorges before merging with the Tuotuo River at Nangjibalong to form what is commonly referred to as the Tongtian River.

The Chumar River, 530.3 kilometers in length.

Chumar in the Tibetan language means "a red-water river"; taking on its characteristic from the silt tributes of the many lakes which pour into it. As the northern source of the Yangtze River, it joins the Tongtian River at Qumalai.

We have followed the drop here to the place that the Tuotuo River, the Dangqu and the Chumar River converge into the Tongtian River. It is from here on that the river becomes known as the great Yangtze!

Chapter Two
A Plateau of Lives

Every prostration on a pilgrimage is a step closer towards the sacred goal.

Every prostration on a pilgrimage is a step closer towards the sacred goal.

Twenty years ago, Tibetan monks followed the Qinghai-Tibet Highway on their pilgrimage to Lhasa. Twenty years later, pilgrims from all over the world are carried by something more in keeping with the times—the Qinghai-Tibet Railroad.

Traversing at an average of 4,500 meters above sea level, this railroad breaks world records in altitude. Known as the "Heavenly Road", it zigzags across the wild "Source of Three Rivers" region; the birthplace of the Yellow River, the Yangtze River and the Lancang River. It covers an area of 318,000 square kilometers. Here, the pristine glaciers, lakes, streams and swamps sustain the livelihood of the three rivers. It is a region with the largest number of natural wetlands and the greatest level of biodiversity among other high-altitude areas in the world.

Kekexili, "a beautiful girl" in Mongolian, covers an area of 83,000 square kilometers on the north-western Qinghai-Tibet Plateau. At an average height of 4,000 meters above sea level, Kekexili is the largest no-man's-land in the world apart from the poles. Here you can view the history of the earth as is it is preserved and experience the last truly virgin lands of China.

The harsh face of Kekexili turns gentle from time to time as it nurtures the

The Qinghai-Tibet Railroad

Chumar River—the northern Yangtze source—and its area of 50,000 square kilometers is home to numerous plateau lakes of various sizes.

The Kekexili region is known for the high density of its plateau lakes. While the mighty Yangtze River, the Yellow River and the Lancang River rush to the east, over 50 seasonal rivers roam freely ranging anywhere from several to scores of kilometers, nourishing life along the way before emptying into lakes.

It is a world of ice and snow almost all year round in Kekexili; too harsh and lonely for human beings, but ideal for wild animals. As winter gives way to spring, wherever there is water in Kekexili—there is life. Migratory birds find their haven in this peaceful plateau of waterways. Wildlife reigns over this vast territory; its grassy shoals and wetlands provide ample food and space for them. At present, there are more than 230 kinds of wild animals in Kekexili. Eleven out of the 29 mammals found on the wasteland here are unique to the Qinghai-Tibet Plateau.

Migratory birds

Longbao Shoal is the first wetland of the source of the Yangtze River.

Flocks of sheep in the "Source of Three Rivers" region

In May each year snow melts for a transient summer on the plateau. As usual, pregnant Tibetan antelopes, a species unique to China known as the "Kekexili Spirit", will embark on a mysterious passage to Kekexili. Just as their ancestors, they travel from their new homelands as far as Qiangtang in Tibet or Arjin in Xinjiang.

The eyes of travellers on this plateau were fixed not only on the gentle beauty of these creatures, but on the value of their "soft gold" fibers. About 100 grams of shahtoosh, the coveted fibers, can be harvested from each Tibetan antelope. A shawl made from the shahtoosh of three to four Tibetan antelopes sells at around US$ 50,000 in the European market. Blinded by such huge gain, poachers arrived and slaughtered innocent Tibetan antelopes in such a frenzy that their numbers dropped from nearly one million to less than 10,000.

The only antelope living at high altitudes on earth; it is now classified as one of the world's Class I Protected Wildlife species. In 1996, environmental protection volunteers set up China's first wildlife protection station along the traditional passageway of these gentle Tibetan antelopes. A telescope on

Sanandaj is China's first wildlife protection station.

the watchtower has a field of vision of 200 kilometers, and after ten years, awareness of the need for protection has increased and poaching has been effectively controlled.

Some age old elements are preserved while other man-made elements are improved upon. In 2004, the newly completed the Tuotuo River Railway Bridge in the river source area replaced the Qinghai-Tibet Highway Bridge once heralded as "The First Bridge Spanning the Yangtze River."

Although this is the mode of passage for men, we shall continue to follow the passageway of the Tibetan antelope round the foot of the highest peak in Kekexili, the Bukadaban. This grand peak sits on the border between Qinghai Province and Xinjiang Autonomous Region. In addition to rivers and lakes, there are thermal springs whose year-round temperatures stand at 91 degrees Celsius.

Wild yaks, the largest animal on the Qinghai-Tibet Plateau, watch those who would intrude upon their territory closely. They merely turn a thoughtful

A Tibetan antelope

Wild yak

The Zhuonai Lake

glance at the Tibetan antelopes making their way hastily across the Kekexili wasteland to reach Zhuonai Lake in time.

Zhuonai Lake, worshipped by some as the Mother Lake, is at its best this time of the year. After marching day and night for two months, tens of thousands of expectant antelopes finally begin to arrive. In a way particular to Tibetan antelopes, early arrivals will not start labor until the sisters from their herds have also arrived.

When night falls, the plateau is usually shrouded in mystery. However, the rangers are full of expectation because they know that tonight, expectant antelopes will deliver. The sky and the earth, the mountains and the lake, are all awaiting the sudden burst of new life. Tonight is a sleepless night. When sun rises in the morning, it will fall upon even newer arrivals.

The newborn lamb

The cries of the newborn lambs, each weighing between 2.8 and 3.3 kilograms, revitalize the Kekexili. In keeping with the determined spirit of this great species, they can stand on their feet before their mother's water dries; walk within 10 minutes of arrival into this world; and gallop within three days.

The Tibetan antelopes are crossing through the Qinghai-Tibet Highway.

With care and protective efforts from people, the population of Tibetan antelopes has gradually gone up to about 50,000. The peaceful pilgrimage of these "Kekexili spirits" remains a celebrated sign of the nation's dedication to preservation.

The Source of Three Rivers region, which the Qinghai-Tibet Railroad traverses, is a major area where wild animals propagate, migrate and feed.

While it was unprecedented in Chinese railroad history for trains to give way to nature, the budget set aside for environmental protection while constructing the Qinghai-Tibet Railroad was RMB 2.1 billion. It is the first railroad to provide no less than 33 wildlife preservation projects along its route, in addition to building a "passage of life" for migrating plateau animals.

The Qinghai-Tibet Railroad also succeeded for the first time in transplanting turf at high altitudes, setting up an exemplary precedent for environmental protection planning on other major Chinese development projects. The completion of the Qinghai-Tibet Railroad will make free flow of goods and people possible in Tibet.

Landscape along the Qinghai-Tibet Railroad has been preserved. The thousand-mile-long tracks have been well merged into the surrounding rivers, snowy mountains and lakes. The developing infrastructure carries us outward and onward just like the Tuotuo River goes on flowing east to join Dangqu, the southern source of the Yangtze River, at Nangjibalong. From this point on, it is

The Labu Village in Yushu District

known as the Tongtian River.

As everyone knows, rivers have always been used as guides for travelling between two distant places. They provided sustenance along the way, and a sure guarantee that one would not lose one's way. There is an ancient path along the ancient Tongtian River. 1,300 years ago, a huge procession of imperial carriages was trekking this desolate path. In the main carriage sat a girl from Chang'an named Xueyan Li, better known as Princess Wencheng.

The effects of this one procession left indelible imprints on this plateau. Wherever she travelled, Princess Wencheng introduced not only Buddhism, but also agricultural civilization. Today farmers on the banks of the Tongtian River in Yushu District are still using ploughs driven by two oxen yoked together, a tool introduced by the Princess.

The lamas of the Labu Temple

The Leba Gorge at Yushu looks exactly the same as it did more than 1,000 years ago. The Princess Wencheng Temple here has been a silent witness to the passage of time.

Jiegu Town, a town of military importance in Qinghai Province, is also the seat of Yushu Tibetan Autonomous Prefecture. Jiegu in Tibetan means "a distribution center." On its way west, the Yangtze River finds Yushu to be the first populous place, birthed undoubtedly by its role in drawing people who traded goods.

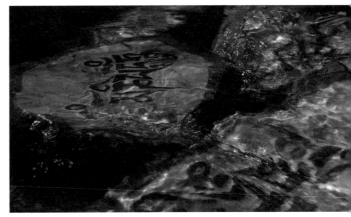

Mani stones are the crafts of Tibetan Buddhism.

An important part of the Source of Three Rivers region, Yushu has a fragile ecosystem because of its high altitude. In recent years, global warming, natural disasters, rampant problems with vermin and over-grazing have reduced some areas here into deserts.

This oasis along Tongtian River is called Labu Village, where white poplar groves survive miraculously at 3,700 meters above sea level. These trees were not native to this area, and lead us to the famous 300-year-old Labu Temple, known throughout Yushu as the home of the Fourth Living Buddha, Jiangyong-luosongjiangcuo. Having once made a pilgrimage to Xining for a Buddhist ceremony, the white poplar trees he saw along the streets prompted him to make a bold decision.

He bought 2,000 saplings with money earned from trading. Although only 60 saplings survived by the end of his long journey back, he was so sincere that it was said that even heaven was moved. These 60 saplings took root at Labu Village, multiplied and spread across the entire prefecture.

It is because of the tree planting practice over the past 100 years that Labu Village has been able to supply clean water day and night to the torrential Tongtian River.

An old man in the mountainous range had a dream in which God revealed that, to ensure the eternal prosperity of the Yangtze and Yellow River source area, the purity of snowy mountains, and the cleanness of lakes that are never to dry up, a hero by the name of Gesar would be born here. The Qinghai-Tibet Plateau is a rich source of legends and ballads as well as rivers. It is here that the saga Gesar was created.

The shelter-forest along the Tongtian River

In 2001, the Chinese government started to develop a 59-kilometer long green corridor on the plateau. At one end of this corridor stands Yushu.

With oases forming, water quality in the Yangtze River has improved, soil erosion reduced, sandiness in the upper reaches of the Yangtze River ameliorated. The ecosystem at the Source of Three Rivers region, also known as "Cistern of China", has come under more effective protection.

There are a lot of folk stone carvers at Yushu. Mani Stones, particular to Tibetan Buddhism on which the six-letter sacred mantra is carved, together with fluttering sutra streamers, are essential components of the unique Qinghai-Tibet culture.

Every year 108 Mani stones are put into the Tongtian River. Local Tibetans believe that they form a golden bridge. Water flows over the "Golden Bridge" towards the sea, bringing with it people's best wishes.

The Tongtian River is renamed Jinsha River after passing Yushu. It surges eastward, vast and mighty.

Chapter Three
Benefiting from the Jinsha River

An ancient ceremony is performed at the ancient town at dawn and dusk every day. Although no one can tell who the ingenious designer was, the ancient streets here are washed anew every time the water gate to the Western River is opened and river water flows rapidly towards the lower-lying eastern part of the town. Each day starts and ends with a street washing. Such a practice at the Square Street of Lijiang seems to be unique in China.

The snow-draped Yulong Mountain soars 5,596 meters into the clouds right to the north of the ancient town. It is this glaciered peak, the closest of its kind to the equator in the world, that provides running water to the ancient town. Melted snow joins spring water at the foot of the mountain to form the 40,000-square-meter Black Dragon Pond, and then flows into the ancient town of Lijiang via the 15-kilometer long Yu River, endowing the town with a fresh look each day.

The ancient town is well sheltered by Yulong Mountain to the north, and the torrential Jinsha River on all three other sides. The Nu River, the Lancang River and the Jinsha River, which all originate from the Qinghai-Tibet Plateau,

Wash the ancient streets of Lijiang in the morning

The snow-draped Yulong Mountain and Lijiang Ancient Town

The First Bend of the Yangtze River

run parallel to each other as they cross the Hengduan Mountains, forming a spectacular view known throughout the world. Of the three, the Nu and the Lancang River follow straighter courses; while the Jinsha River, the upper reaches of the Yangtze, makes a U-turn outside Lijiang. This is the First Bend of the Yangtze River.

It is this bend that determines the eastward course of the Yangtze River, creating the Tiger Leaping Gorge between Yulong Mountain and Haba Mountain. A spectacular 18-kilometer long gorge with seven waterfalls and 18 dangerous shoals, it is the deepest and steepest in the world.

The Jingsha River

Such natural wonders as snowy mountains, the Jinsha River and spring water joined hands in creating the miracle of Lijiang. The gold deposits in the Jinsha River gave Lijiang its name, because according to ancient Chinese classics, "Gold is found in beautiful rivers," and Lijiang in Chinese means "a beautiful river."

The ancient Town of Lijiang

There were less than 300,000 inhabitants in the over 800-year old Lijiang. These days, however, more than three millions visitors from home and abroad crowd its streets every year.

A major earthquake in 1996 drew even greater world attention to Lijiang. Seeing the steady stream of visitors, some local inhabitants decided to turn their houses into family hotels.

Newcomers complain about the labyrinthine streets and alleys at Lijiang. Unlike other ancient towns, Lijiang has no central axle, no symmetric layout, few straight roads, and it is hard to tell direction. But all these only make the ancient town even more fascinating.

Streets and houses have been built along waterways. It was these crisscrossing waterways that turn the alleys into a labyrinth, but no one knows when they were dug or who dug them. Likewise, no one can tell how many creeks there are in this ancient town.

Only one thing is certain, that in the very beginning there was only one creek in the ancient town, which flowed in from the northern side and out of the south-eastern side before joining the Jinsha River. Afterwards, people dug out an Eastern River and a Western River out of what later became known as

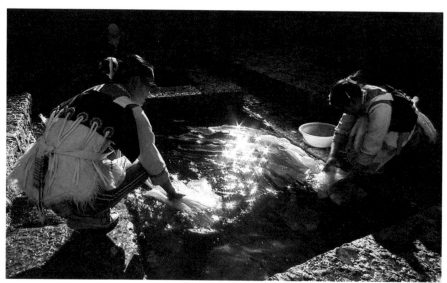

The Three Wells

the Central River. Afterwards more branches were hewn to the point that by the Qing Dynasty Lijiang had become a town cradled by water.

Residents of Lijiang regard wells in the town, which are found almost everywhere, as its eyes. The wells are in fact mouths of springs. It is those scattered wells, the cobweb of creeks, plus the Central River, the Eastern Western Rivers, which complete the complicated and ingeniously designed water system in town. Wells usually appear in threes, cascading from one to another. The age-old practice is to draw drinking water from the top well, wash vegetables in the middle one, and do laundry in the bottom well.

There are now more than 260 family hotels in the ancient town. Guests are always curious about the famous "Jishasha". In this ancient Naxi word was first symbolized in the ancient hieroglyph used by Dongba's, "ji" refers to water inside a house, and "shasha", two locks. So "jishasha" means locking up auspicious water inside the house.

A Dongba was a term first coined to describe a Naxi priest, and then later the term for the written language exclusively used by Dongba's; the best preserved and most ancient hieroglyphs in the world.

However, other people believe "Jishasha" was actually the term for the sound of the gurgling water which is heard everywhere in the ancient town.

There is a beautiful story behind each beautiful place name. This ancient town got its name from its continuous flow of water. Abundant water has

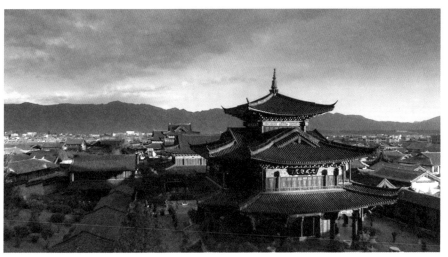

The residence of the Mu Chieftain in Lijiang

attracted Naxi people, generations of whom have committed themselves to the well-being of Lijiang. At present, Naxi population still dominates this flat land between the Jinsha River and Yulong Mountain where a dozen ethnic groups live. What's more, 30% of the Naxi residents still practice traditional forms of handicrafts.

Since ancient times Lijiang has been an important stop on an ancient trading route, known as the Tea Caravan Route. The route was carved by countless human feet and horse hooves that trekked the rugged grounds where three great rivers run parallel to each other.

Evidence shows that it is highly likely that this ancient route came into

Dongba hieroglyph inscriptions and the Jishasha family hotel

Bridge in Lijiang

being as early as the Tang Dynasty. Since caravans need stop from time to time, towns emerged along the route.

Lijiang became a natural stop because it was situated on flat land with abundant water. Caravans arrived from all directions before dispersing in all directions. As a result the Square Street became the town center, from which streets and houses radiate.

The ancient town at Lijiang is still alive today. Covering a modest area of 3.8 square kilometers, it looks like a huge ink slab when viewed from above, hence its other name "Great Ink-Slab Town."

Traders in caravans have become history. In their place nowadays it is backpackers who crowd the streets of Lijiang.

Locals can't help worrying that the huge number of tourists may disrupt the pace of life here, or even destroy its primitive simplicity. They have started to take care to preserve tradition.

From the largest stone bridge to a two-meter long plank, there are in total 354 bridges at Lijiang; a national record for bridge density. There used to be such a bridge in Northern Lijiang with a novel name, "Bridge above Water, and Water on Bridge."

The bridge is gone, but older local residents still remember it as a flood control mechanism. Flood water was first diverted onto this bridge, and then into the Central River, where the huge amount of rapidly flowing river water would carry it out of the town. It is such a clever use of the water system in town that has kept the ancient town as well as its water system safe.

This bronze statue at Xueding Temple outside the ancient town is the Water God worshipped by Naxi people. Naxi people believe that man is part of nature just like all other things on earth, and that like man everything else on earth has a soul. Therefore they are devout worshippers of mountains, caretakers of plants and trees, and of course admirers of water, something that has been with them in better and in worse, a great gift by nature, the soul of Lijiang.

The elder residents in Lijiang

It was out of a sense of mission that those old hands in music reunited. Now in their seventies, those former teachers, tailors and caravan leaders have been sending shock waves across the world after their first original ancient Naxi concert in 1981.

Hailing from Tang and Song Dynasties and impregnated with Taoist charm, ancient music lost to the Central Plains was heard all over Lijiang at night, a second life thanks to these old Naxi musicians. Some say that although this is not music recorded in history or performed at grand theaters, musicians in the band may be as great as Johann Sebastian Bach, though far less well known.

Contented with life, Lijiang people respect their tradition and nature; therefore the values embedded in the ancient town are keys to their existence and the continuation of their way of life.

Harmony between man and nature is flowing day in, day out in Lijiang; a place that has been giving out best wishes to people as well as receiving them. Those best wishes will be carried by its springs and creeks to Jinsha River, and along to the Yangtze River close by.

Chapter Four
Eastbound

Lijiang was named after the Lishui River, which became known as the "Jinsha" meaning "gold deposits". During the Song Dynasty when gold was found on its 2,308–meter long river bed, people believed it to be a tributary of the Yangtze River.

In 1639, Xu Xiake, who was in his fifties, came to Lijiang. It was to be his last journey to identify a river source. His geological expedition changed the long established perception of the Yangtze River, and pointed out directions for future explorations. Ever since then the Jinsha River has been regarded as the upper reaches of Yangtze's mainstream. It was nearly 300 years later that modern expeditions finally trekked far enough along the Jinsha River to locate the source of the Yangtze.

Melted glacier waters at Gela Dandong gave birth to numerous narrow creeks. They form the head stream of the Yangtze River, known to locals as the Tuotuo River. There is a vivid term in physiognomy for such an extraordinary cobweb of creeks - a braided water system.

The Tuotuo River travels over 370 kilometers before joining the Dangqu River to flow southeast in the course of the Tongtian River. After rambling another 813 kilometers the Tongtian River merges into the Jinsha River at the Batang River estuary at Yushu, Qinghai Province.

The Batang River estuary is the dividing point for the Tongtian River and the Jinsha River, but for the Yangtze River it assumes a far greater significance than a change of name. After the Batang River estuary, the Yangtze River flows into the Hengduan Mountains that run generally from north to south. As a result, the Yangtze River flows eastward along the Tongtian River section but southward in the Jinsha River section. Its unbridled watercourse in the open

The Jingsha River

country turns into an ice-breaking journey through lofty mountains and precipitous gorges.

A unique natural wonder was born in the mysterious Hengduan Mountain range and extends for over a thousand miles. Along the mountains the Nu, Lancang and the Jinsha Rivers, each great in its own rite, run parallel from northwest to southeast for more than 1,000 kilometers. Sometimes they are as close as nineteen kilometers from each other, but they never converge, hence the geological wonder. In July 2007 this area of racing "brother" rivers became a World Natural Heritage site. Then how did such a wonder come into being?

About 40 million years ago major mountain formation started around the Himalayas. A series of folds that run from northwest to southeast were formed when two land masses began to collide with each other, steering the water system in their gorges accordingly, hence the miracle of the "three parallel rivers."

Major geological upheavals have left deep impressions in the area, making it a historical textbook on the evolution of earth in the eyes of scientists. Among all geological wonders here, the most awe-inspiring is the ferric oxide-rich Danxia landform that covers a total area of 250 square kilometers. It is the largest and the best developed Danxia landform in China.

The Danxia landform in the Source of Three Rivers region

Here the Yangtze River flows the most rapidly. In a narrow stretch just thirty meters wide and sixteen kilometers long the Jinsha River falls 213 meters. A difference in elevation of over 3,900 meters between mountain top and river surface makes the Tiger Leaping Gorge one of the deepest gorges on earth.

Swift river water tears through towering ridges. Down from the Tiger Leaping Gorge the snowy Yulong Mountain and Haba Mountain part curtains for the Jinsha River, which rushes relentlessly towards the east. In the past the rapid currents across a narrow river surface made the Jinsha River an almost insurmountable natural barrier.

The only place to cross the Jinsha River lies over 20 kilometers up the Tiger Leaping Gorge, where mountain formation events in ancient times forced the Jinsha River to make a 270-degree turn from its original course towards the southeast, slowing down the rushing water.

The Tiger Leaping Gorge

In 1253 A.D., Kublai Khan led 100,000 soldiers on an expedition to Yunnan. It was here that they crossed the Jinsha River in skin rafts made out of entire sheets of oxen or goat skin and united China. This famous military manoeuvre has become known as "Mongols Crossing the River in Skin Rafts." Locals there continued to use

Skin rafts were used to cross rivers in the 1920s and 1930s.

the same type of skin rafts to cross the river even as late as the 1920s and 1930s.

Although people today cross the peaceful looking river in engine-powered ferries, they find the journey far from a piece of cake, because the current flows at an astounding speed of 4 meters per second.

The U-turn made here by the Jinsha River is the famous "First Bend of the Yangtze River." Adjacent to the Bend is Stone Drum Town, a former key post along the Tea Caravan Route in Yunnan, whose past glory is inscribed on a drum-shaped white marble tablet.

Ancient merchants travelling between Tibet and better developed regions in China traded in the town fair, but now the town finds most of its visitors to be tourists wanting to view the "First Bend of the Yangtze River" through their own eyes. It is here that the Yangtze River parts company with the Nu and Lancang Rivers and makes its critical eastbound turn. The series of cragged mountains

Stone Drum Town and the drum-shaped stone tablet

around the Tiger Leaping Gorge are the first barrier it has to overcome before flowing east towards the sea.

300 kilometers outside of the ancient town of Lijiang, the Jinsha River reaches Sichuan Province. What used to be a ferry crossing just twenty years ago is now as bustling as any other city. This is Panzhihua, the youngest city on the Jinsha River.

Thanks to its considerable iron ore reserve, Panzhihua has attracted many workers from all over China to become a city of over one million people in 40 years' time. Here, the Yalong River, the longest tributary of the Yangtze River, joins the Jinsha. The former originates from Bayankela Mountain in Qinghai Province, dropping roughly 4,420 meters over its gorge-lined journey of 1,637 kilometers.

The Ertan Hydropower Station was completed in 2000 in the lower reaches of the Yalong River. About thirty kilometers from downtown Panzhihua, it was China's largest hydropower station before the Three Gorges Dam project started.

Here the Jinsha River breaks away from snowy mountains towards a new zone—the hot, dry river valley area. Owing to meteorological and topographical reasons Panzhihua boasts the largest primeval cycad forest in the world.

The rapid currents and numerous reefs in the Jinsha River make Panzhihua inaccessible by water. Yibin is the city furthest up the Yangtze River to be reached by ships. Shipping on the Yangtze River starts here, making Yibin the "First City on the Yangtze River." Since the major portion of the 1,030-meter long river course running from Yibin, Sichuan Province to Yichang, Hubei Province is located within Sichuan Province, people often call it the "Sichuan River". The 4,500-meter mainstream from the river source to Yichang is referred to as the upper reaches of the Yangtze River.

Two more tributaries merge into the Yangtze River at Yibin. They are

The city of Panzhihua

The Ertan Hydropower Station on the Yalong River

the Min River from the northern bank and the Nanguang River from the south. Although the latter, rising from Yunnan Province, is dwarfed by many other major tributaries along the upper reaches of the Yangtze River, it was of strategic importance to the feudal monarchy in the Central Plains. When time came to expand to the south-western frontier or to facilitate trade between north-eastern Yunnan and Sichuan or other provinces along the Yangtze River, the Nanguang played a key role in coordinating movements.

In the past ships travelling on the Nanguang River would stop by a "River Gate" when they reached Yibin, and then discharge passengers or cargo into the city. Established in 182 B.C., the city of Yibin utilized the Yangtze and Min Rivers strategically as moats by building its walls on river banks. City gates on all four sides are actually "River Gates".

Yibin is surrounded by the Min River, the tributary with the largest water volume along the upper reaches of the Yangtze River. It travels 735 kilometers through the region in Sichuan Basin where the precipitation is the highest while attracting several tributaries of its own, such as the Dadu and Qingyi Rivers. Previously regarded as the head stream of the Yangtze River, it originates from the southern side of the Min Mountains in Aba, Sichuan Province.

After flowing south into the Sichuan Basin, the Min River is divided into an inner part and outer part to the north of Qingcheng Mountain, a famous Taoist attraction. There the Dujiang Weirs, China's most famous irrigation network, gave birth to Chengdu, the land of plenty. Of all rivers in China, the Min River possesses the greatest number of World Heritage sites due to its long standing role in the nation's history and culture.

The Min River drainage area is located mainly within the boundaries of Sichuan Basin, one of the four largest basins in China. Covering an area of 200,000 square kilometers, this basin is almost completely isolated from the rest of the world by mountains on all four sides. There is an abundance of water resource in Sichuan, with more than 1,000 rivers, great or small, nourishing the land. Water brings tenderness and suppleness to Sichuan Basin. An aerial view of the basin proves the vital role played by water in this land of plenty. Its abundant water and nurturing climate make the Sichuan Basin the richest land in western China.

The name "Sichuan", meaning "four rivers" was derived from the four great rivers here: the Min River, Tuo, Jialing and Wu Rivers.

The Jialing River, which originates from Qinling, Shaanxi Province, got its name from the Jialing Valley it flows through in Feng County, Shaanxi Province. 1,120 kilometers in length and 160,000 square kilometers in total area, it has the largest drainage area of all tributaries of the Yangtze River. Chongqing, the largest city in the upper reaches of the Yangtze River, is located where the Jialing River merges into the Yangtze River. Yuzhong Peninsula, a 22 square-kilometer area enclosed by the two rivers, is Chongqing's hub of trade, commerce, finance and transportation.

The width of the Yangtze River in Sichuan Province is determined by the surrounding terrain. It is at its widest where the Wu River comes in from the southern bank, or the Fuling District of Chongqing. 1,037 kilometers in length, the Wu River originates from Wumeng Mountains, traverses mid-Guizhou from southwest to northeast, and joins the Yangtze River at Fuling. The Wu River is the largest tributary south of the upper reaches of the Yangtze River. Up until a half century ago it had been most essential to the exchange of commodities between Guizhou Province and other parts of the country.

Of all the tributaries of the Yangtze River, the Wu River is known as an eco-river because of its well-preserved vegetation. Moreover, the surrounding mountains block steam from the river surface, making the temperature, humidity and illumination here ideal for the growth of mustard tuber, thereby winning Fuling the good name of the "Home of Hot Pickled Mustard Tuber." The Chinese like this food grown widely in south-western China so much that they have taken it with them wherever they went.

Along the 1,000-kilometer course the Yangtze River absorbs a dozen tributaries, with notable contributors such as the Yalong, Min, Chishui, Tuo, Qi, Jialing and Wu Rivers. Wherever there is a convergence, there is a city; examples of convincing evidence that civilization is created alongside water.

With each joining tributary, the Yangtze water volume and force of flow increases. As a result it surges ahead, coming alive with greater and greater energy.

These river-locking columns, formerly numbering seven, were erected on both banks of the Yangtze River in the late South Song Dynasty more than 700 years ago. In times of war huge iron chains were tossed across the river and tied to iron columns there to block enemy battleships, making it very hard to capture.

The river-locking columns are found at the Kuimen part of the Three Gorges area, the vital passage into Sichuan. It is so precipitous here that at the narrowest there are only scores of meters between two banks.

After Kuimen the Yangtze River again flows into gorges. Rolling mountain ranges, complex geological structures and torrential water join hands to create the greatest spectacle on the Yangtze River—the Three Gorges. The Qutang, Wu and Xiling Gorges along the 208-kilometer section stretch between Fengjie, Chongqing and Yichang, Hubei Province.

Since its origin on Qinghai-Tibet Plateau, the Yangtze River has been adhering unswervingly to its course towards the sea. When blocked by the Wu Mountains, it exerts energy it gathered so far to split them transversely, creating a show of its

A distant view of the Qutang Gorge

Nanjin Pass is where the Three Gorges area ends.

power. Eventually it finally overcomes the second major barrier towards the East Sea and leaves behind the enchanting sceneries of the Three Gorges.

This 8,000-meter gorge between Kuimen and Daxi Town, Wushan County is the Qutang Gorge, the first of the Three Gorges. Although the shortest, it is regarded as the most majestic. The scenery is the most striking where the Wu Mountains appear to have been torn apart by the Yangtze River.

The 45-kilometer long Wu Gorge is the longest of the three, known for its profound serenity and changeable weather. There are twelve 1,000-meter-or-above stand-alone peaks in the Wu Gorge Area, hence the name the "Twelve Peaks of the Wu Mountains". Romantic legends about the Goddess of the Wu Mountains have developed out of those peaks that are always shrouded in mist.

Despite the fact that the Xiling Gorge is the widest of the three, currents here are so rapid that it is also the most dangerous. Since the Three Gorges Dam was erected, the water level here has risen, and the water flow tempered. As Mao Zedong wrote in his poem, "a smooth lake has risen in the narrow gorges."

A cruise boat named after the Goddess of the Wu Mountains was launched in 1981 to take people on a tour of the Three Gorges. Passengers more than twenty years ago watched boat trackers on the river banks while awed by the spectacular scenery.

Since the Three Gorges Dam was put to use, the water level has risen so much that sightseers today can reach deep into the gorges. Only in the most

The Daning River (after the water level of Three Gorges Dam raised)

remote gorges are boat trackers still working. The last generation of boat trackers along the Yangtze River has become a valued part of the preservation of ancient civilization and savage beauty that attracts tourists from near and afar.

The construction of Gezhouba Dam, the first dam on the Yangtze River, filled the local people with pride. It helped set the stage for the development of the Three Gorges Dam, China's largest ever water control project.

The Three Gorges Dam is located at Sandouping; a mere 38 kilometers up the Yangtze River from Gezhouba Dam. Yichang, Hubei Province sits on the dividing line between the upper reaches and the middle-to-lower reaches of the Yangtze River. With two dams within the boundaries of Yichang, the city stands out from its peers on the Yangtze River as a major hydroelectric powerhouse for the country.

The upper reaches stretch 4,500 kilometers from the snow-draped Gela Dandong to Yichang, two thirds of the total length of the Yangtze River. On its way across China's three major terraces the great river falls a total of 5,400 kilometers, tearing its way through mountain barriers; proof enough that hard rocks are no match for gentle but tenacious river water.

The Three Gorges area ends at Nanjin Pass, a miraculous divide between rolling mountains to the west and vast open country to the east. After conquering Nanjin Pass the Yangtze River is finally released to follow its will eastbound towards to sea.

Chapter Five
Ages of Water

The point where the Bai River and the Jialing River converge

Two creeks run close to each other, but never join until some 400 kilometers downstream when they approach a major river. This clear tributary merges into the Jialing River, which originates from Shaanxi Province, at Aba Tibetan and Qiang Autonomous Prefecture before emptying into the Yangtze River.

If one walks up this clear tributary towards its source, one will find the famous Jiuzhaigou and Huanglonggou valleys, famous for their lakes and mystical waterfalls. Legend has it that the lakes were slivers of a mirror that was broken by a fairy. The widest legend tells that the mirror was broken into 108 pieces, therefore there are 108 lakes scattered in the remote mountains and verdant valleys of Jiuzhaigou.

Although variations of the number of pieces sprung up over the years: some say 108 pieces, 114 pieces, or 118 pieces, but the consistent thread is the unusual fact that the lakes are different in size, shape, type of water, and color. Secluded in the mountains seldom frequented by man, those slivers of the fairy mirror reflect the tranquillity of their surrounding.

About 1,000 years ago, ancestors of the modern day Jiuzhaigou residents moved here from the war-torn Qinghai-Tibet Plateau. They set up nine hamlets in the valley including Shuzheng, Heye and Zharu—hence the name Jiuzhaigou, meaning "a valley of nine hamlets" in Chinese.

108 lakes in Shuzheng

How could Jiuzhaigou, this water fairyland extending fifty kilometers and covering an area of 720 square kilometers between the south-eastern edge of the Qinghai-Tibet Plateau and the Min Mountains have remained hidden? It impressively blends with the Shuzheng, Rize and Zezhawa Valleys which are 52% luxuriant primeval forests. Until loggers discovered it in 1956, this area remained unknown and undisturbed.

Two forest resource investigators broke through brambles and thorns of the Min Mountains and chanced upon this forbidden land of fairies. Jiuzhaigou, a haven to rare fauna and flora, was discovered and unveiled to the world. Over 2,000 botanic species and more than 300 zoological species, many of them rarely seen outside, had been living a quiet life for generations.

Abundant water nourishes the primeval forest covering an area of 300 square kilometers ranging in elevation from 3,100 to 2,000 meters. The forest puts on varied looks at different altitudes during different seasons, like a lady changing her wardrobe.

In January each year, the temperature drops to below 20 degrees

The river way of Peacock River

The Long Lake

The Nuorilang Waterfall

Celsius, freezing lakes and even the majestic Nuorilang Waterfall. In this world of ice and snow only the magical Five Flowers Lake is still flowing.

Situated at 2,472 meters above sea level, the 80,000-square-meter Five Flowers Lake maintains a water temperature of six degrees Celsius in freezing weather, thanks to the many gurgling hot springs scattered on its bottom some twenty meters below surface that contribute 30% of the liquid in Five Flowers Lake. Apart from rainfall, where does the lake acquire such a huge volume? Water from the melted snow of the surrounding mountains is constantly injected into this lake.

The 930,000-square-meter Long Lake at 3,100 meters above sea level is the highest and largest lake in Jiuzhaigou.

At first glance there is no outlet for the Long Lake; however, cracks between the mountain folds are quietly and ceaselessly channelling water into the lower-lying lakes and waterways of Jiuzhaigou.

Calcium carbonate sediments are present here in and out of water, a typical characteristic of karsts topography. Together with the omnipresent running water they created the beautiful scenery in Jiuzhaigou.

These artistic markings in the sediment are vestiges of earth's Fourth Ice Age about three million years ago. Before that time they simply drifted with water, but about 12,000 years ago when earth warmed up they shook off inertia and started to attach to objects wherever water carried them. About half a century ago when they made their debut, the formations were polished enough to astound the world. Yet in geology the formation process is by no

The pagodas in Jiuzhaigou

means picturesque, those "barrier" lakes were created out of water gathered within piled-up calcium carbonate deposits.

Blockage gave birth to lakes connected by cascading waterfalls. Now here, now there, water meanders through the calcium carbonate formations, leaving people to marvel at the miracles performed.

Most residents in Jiuzhaigou are Tibetans, the offspring of early immigrants enchanted by the sacred mountains and lakes. It seems that that their life is always related to the abundant water; be it for farming, grazing or powering water mills.

It was beyond their wildest imaginations that so many people would visit with them, or that their homestead would wow the outside world, altering their lives so profoundly.

In 1992 Jiuzhaigou became a World Natural Heritage site; in 1998, UNESCO included it in the MAB Biosphere Reserve Directory. It was the first Tibetan recluse of its kind to be included to better protect the many rare fauna and flora.

Close to the Min Mountains and

Jiuzhaigou people

The Twirling Flower Pond

about 140 kilometers from Jiuzhaigou is the famous Huanglonggou. This tranquil spring nestled against the 5,000-odd-meter Jade Peak is sacred to Tibetans. They often come here to offer flowers to their gods. If petals swirl in the spring, then the gods have accepted their sacrifice. Therefore the spring is named the "Twirling Flower Pond".

Despite its modest length of less than 4 kilometers, the 3,000-odd-meter Huanglonggou boasts over 3,400 colorful ponds. What surprises people the most is that all water flowing in Huanglonggou is actually supplied by the little "Twirling Flower Pond" where people pray.

For ages Huanglonggou maintained its virgin look as a holy place to local Tibetans as it was off limits to outsiders. The pale yellow tufa accumulated on the ground turns the over 3,000 colorful ponds into what appears like

The Huanglonggou

The Min Mountains

Calcify stone bamboo shoots

layers upon layers of scales glistening in the sun. When viewed from above, the entire Huanglonggou resembles a crouching golden dragon, hence the name "Huanglonggou", which means "Yellow Dragon Gorge" in Chinese.

300 million years ago, the entire Min Mountain range, together with Jiuzhaigou and Huanglonggou, were covered beneath a deep ocean. As major mountain building activities elevated the Qinghai-Tibet Plateau, the Min Mountains also rose from the sea bottom into a huge range with the highest peak standing at 5,588 meters above sea level.

Melted snow from towering mountains filtered its way through the limestone of the mountain, washing out huge amounts of calcium carbonate that was deposited as the water flowed down slopes, wrapping rocks and tree roots on the way. Some was absorbed; some piled up to form ponds, and then shoals. Such a phenomenon was named by scholars as the "Min Mountains Tufa Karst Topography".

Such karst topography is unique in the world, and the resulting sceneries in Huanglonggou and Jiuzhaigou are the world's finest.

Like an artist's palette, the 693 ponds, each with its own unique shade of color, link with each other to form the 20,000-square-meter Five Color Ponds area; the largest cluster of colorful ponds in Huanglonggou.

Scientific explorers in Jiuzhaigou discovered that the calcium carbonate

The Five Flowers Lake

concentration in water increases twenty-fold as it flows from the Long Lake to the Five Flowers Lake. Year in, year out, calcium carbonate has been depositing itself non-stop and transforming Jiuzhaigou. According to a simulation done by Dr. Holger Perner, the Five Color Pond expands three millimeters every year. The Min Mountain's karst topography has been thus formed, little by little, with each day's new artwork nearly unnoticed by those who view it.

The stone tower in the midst of the lake was said to be the tomb of the offspring of a meritorious official in the Ming Dynasty. In less than 500 years' time, it has nearly transformed into a calcium carbonate statue.

Now real, now illusory, there is surprise everywhere when it comes to the scenery here: how fast and to what degree is the transformation still going on?

Here nature has given full play to its creativity, eroding the Min Mountains with a constant flow of water, painting with colorful strokes, and leaving mankind with two precious legacies—Jiuzhaigou and Huanglonggou.

The Huanglonggou Natural Preserve is located in Songpan County, Aba Tibetan and Qiang Autonomous Prefecture of Sichuan Province, where two major tributaries of the Yangtze—the Min and Fu Rivers—originate. The ancient town of Songpan lies between

The stone pagoda of Ming Dynasty in the Five Flowers Lake

The ancient town Songpan

Huanglonggou and Jiuzhaigou.

The ancient town of Songpan, a town of significance in the days of the Tea Caravan Route, used to be a hub for inbound and outbound traders. Travellers of a different sort flood Songpan now; in peak seasons the more than 100 tour guides and over 200 horses here can hardly handle the flow of sightseers, including some 8,000 from foreign lands.

Caravans of the past never set foot on Huanglonggou or Jiuzhaigou. Instead they proceeded by way of Munigou, although the routes are of similar length. Also situated in the Huanglonggou Natural Preserve, Munigou is smaller than Huanglonggou but more primitive since traces of human presence are few.

It was on this huge limestone fossil in Munigou that ecologists discovered clear traces of water flow on the eroded surface. Different in thickness, these layers are growth rings formed in certain time periods, helpful in deducing the speed and process of tufa deposition. It is a pity that the top layer of the decayed tufa has been damaged too much for ecologists to ascertain when it decayed.

Munigou was in its prime for tufa formation 5,000 years ago until a severe earthquake caused lakes to cave in and diverted water flow. As a result some lakes gradually ran dry.

Long term exposure eroded and oxidized the top layer of the tufa, which in turn blackened and aged, eventually dissolving into soil that nourished huge forests.

The Xuebao Peak is the main peak of Min Mountains.

The Tibetans keep steadily maintaining their lifestyle although their homesteads are attracting worldwide attention today. Since Jiuzhaigou and Huanglonggou became natural preserves, they have been protected. The life force of the water replenishes the lakes, forests and every other inch of the land here. To the Tibetans living in Aba, this will always be a Pure Land.

According to their belief, water is the divine spirit that ensures good crops and wellbeing. Every year Tibetans living in Jiuzhaigou and Huanglonggou stage formal ceremonies to invoke the holy mountains and holy water. To them, everything has been endowed by nature.

In Jiuzhaigou and Huanglonggou, water sustains as well as creates beauty. After working wonders here, water flows out of the remote mountains into the Yangtze River several hundred kilometers away.

The traveling caravans along the river

Chapter Six
The Bronze Age

Yueliangwan Village in Guanghan, Deyang on the Chengdu Plain of Sichuan Province is part of the ancient Sanxingdui Remains. Mysteries that remain to be explored underground began to unfold with a major discovery in 1986.

In midsummer 1986 as farmers were digging earth to bake bricks near a mound known as Sanxingdui in Yueliangwan Village, Guanghan, some broken jade pieces suddenly surfaced. A little farther down an odd-looking sculpture of a head appeared.

Exciting archaeological excavations started on July 19th 1986. Awe-inspiring head sculptures of deities were unearthed one after another. Their characteristics were so rare and terrestrial that even well-informed archaeologists were at a loss.

Eleven years later a gigantic museum was erected beside the site to display those extraordinary relics to the public. They are indescribably mysterious to visitors who make all sorts of conjectures on the basis of their own life and experiences.

According to the official reports the 1986 excavation unearthed over 1,000 objects made of bronze, jade, gold, earth, stone and ivory. Archaeologists believe that these relics relate to an unknown civilization or society. The report named the civilization "Sanxingdui Civilization" after the place where it is located. Shortly afterwards, the news spread

The first importance excavation of Sanxingdui in 1986

around the world. Astounded international media and academia started to mention this discovery in the same breath as the ancient civilizations in Egypt, Babylon, Greece and Maya; nominating it as the Ninth Wonder of the World.

Only part of one of the three mounds (Sanxingdui meaning "three mounds" in Chinese) remains today. Ever since the 1986 excavation, many more ancient objects have been discovered by farmers in the roughly twelve square kilometers area around Sanxingdui. Within that area are five villages of Nanxing Town and Three Star Town of Guanghan County.

It is the northern tip of the vast Chengdu Plain, an alluvium of the Min and Tuo River water systems. Thanks to the abundant water supply, this land has been known throughout history as the land of plenty. Culturally and materially wealthy, it still displays traces of ancient dynasties.

The recorded history of the Chengdu Plain dates back more than 2,000 years. Before those records, it was a fertile land in which myths and legends were born.

Many important water systems in the upper reaches of the Yangtze River are here. Before the Ming Dynasty geologist Xu Xiake identified the Jinsha River as the head stream of the Yangtze, the Min River had been regarded as the authentic source. The discovery of the Sanxingdui drew people's attention once again to this river that has many times the water flow of the Yellow River.

In early spring 1929 people were busy with ploughing and sowing. On this particular day when farmer Yan Daocheng and his son dug irrigation channels near where they lived in Yueliangwan Village, Guanghan, they chanced upon some ancient jade pieces. When the shock of finding such valuable pieces was

The Yan Family: Yan Daocheng (father) and Yan Qingbao (son)

The excavation site of Yan Family's residence in 1934

The changing of the character "Shu"

over, father and son returned home and hid them.

Two years later, a British missionary by the name of V.H.Donnithorne came to Guanghan. Upon hearing the story he managed to get hold of some pieces from the Yan family, which he later gave to David Graham, an American anthropologist teaching at West China Union University in Chengdu. In 1934, the latter led an archaeological team to the Yan compound. During the first dig he unearthed more than 600 cultural relics. For some reason, the digging terminated a dozen days later.

At nearly the same time as the Yan family discovery, the first modern excavation by Chinese archaeologists was launched at the Yellow River Basin. They changed the record of world history when they unearthed a legendary dynasty at the Yin ruins—the Shang Dynasty. It was the oldest empire ever discovered up to that time. The excavation of the Yin ruins has been going on ever since 1928. So far over sixty grand palaces and ancestral temples and nearly 1,000 pits for sacrifices have been unearthed. There are remains of horses and carriages and evidence that the dynasty had a custom for burying people and animals alive with the dead. In addition, tens of thousands of pieces of bronze ware, countless tortoise shells and animal bones have been discovered. The ruins cover an area of more than 300,000 square meters.

The discoveries at the Yin Ruins moved back China's recorded history to more than 3,000 years. Together with Yangshao Civilization and Longshan Civilization that were later discovered in the Yellow River Basin, it established the academic belief at that time that the Chinese civilization had started in the Yellow River Basin.

During the excavations at the Yin ruins in the 20th century, much historic information was gathered from the interpretation of unearthed inscriptions on tortoise shells and animal bones, the earliest written language in China. Researchers found many of the several thousand characters they had recognized corresponded to the modern Chinese character "Shu", which means Sichuan or an ancient kingdom in Sichuan. They believed the hieroglyphic character was a combination of the shape of an eye and that of a silkworm. In annals that read almost like myths, people in the land of "Shu" had column-shaped eyes and raised silkworms. Due to the lack of archaeological evidence back then, this ancient kingdom in the upper reaches of the Yangtze River remained illusory.

Archaeological excavation findings that may appear insignificant often signal something profound. In the early 1970s, some 7.000 year old grains of rice rewrote Chinese history. In the lower reaches of the Yangtze River at Hemudu Village, Yuyao County of Zhejiang Province archaeologists discovered the remains of another ancient civilization. Scientific tests determine that as early as six to seven thousand years ago, Hemudu residents grew rice and built houses more than 1,000 years earlier than the Yangshao Civilization in the Yellow River Basin. They were the first in Chinese architecture to use tenons and mortises as evidenced by the complicated large-scale wood structures they built. The discovery of the Hemudu ruins led historians to reset their original dating of the origin of the Chinese civilization some 2,000 years earlier.

Liangzhu Civilization, which dates back to the Neolithic Age over 5,000 years ago, was another major archaeological discovery close to the Hemudu ruins and renowned for its incomparably exquisite jade ware. Experts attribute Liangzhu Civilization, which had a primitive form of a nation state, to the tribe of Chi You who fought against Huangdi to a tragic end. "Huangdi" or "Yellow Emperor" was the legendary ruler and ancestor of what has been considered Chinese civilization.

In the middle-to-late 20th century, archaeologists raised the possibility that the Chinese civilization might have more than one origin when they drew public attention to ancient ruins they had discovered on the middle reaches of the Yangtze River. However, conclusive evidence had not yet been found of the existence of the ancient Shu kingdom.

The 1986 excavation at Sanxingdui

The restored picture of the daily life of Sanxingdui ancestors

The unearthed bronze head sculpture with protruding cylindrical eyes of Sanxingdui

is the largest of its kind, during which a milestone discovery of two sacrificial pits was made. Before that milestone excavation, archaeologists had been searching up and down the plain for half a century with no proof for their hypothesis.

Only a word or two was mentioned about the ancient Shu kingdom in historical annals. Once unearthed, the bronze masks with column-shaped eyes reminded people of ancient literature that was either forgotten or dismissed as improbable. According to legend, the fist king of the ancient Shu kingdom was Cancong, a man with cylindrical shaped pupils obtruding from his eyes.

It was believed that other similarities that characterized Shu people arose from their environment. In ancient times in Sichuan, the sun was always blocked by rains and mists, and trees soared into the skies. Experts believe that people depicted with protruding cylindrical eyes are mystified ancestors of the ancient Shu residents. They had these oddly shaped eyes because their offspring hoped to see beyond the mists.

The ancient Shu kingdom mystified in ancient texts arose from oblivion all of a sudden. Behind those masks there seem to be familiar stories and familiar lives, yet they were so strange, so out of reach. What were once small entries here and there with no threads to follow to confirm, became something tangible; that extraordinary discovery opened the door to a mysterious ancient kingdom. The dwellers who used those excavated objects lived at almost the same time as the Shang Dynasty in the Yellow River Basin. In the historical records referencing Sichuan before its capture by the Qin Dynasty, it had always been a barbarous wilderness. This is the most intriguing element of the discovery of the highly advanced Sanxingdui Civilization; though we see the evidence, it even stretches the belief of some living today.

From top left to below right: bronze vessel, the head of bronze snake, tiger-shaped bronze artifact, bronze scallop-shaped decoration unearthed at Sanxingdui

While all kinds of intricate bronze ware, jade ware, gold artefacts and pottery help recreate devout and magnificent ceremonies of the past, they also disclose the intimate and enjoyable sides of their everyday life. The huge amount of ivories and seashells not only delineate the environment in which ancient Shu people lived, but also the wide extent of their trade and commerce.

People living on this land over 3,000 years ago possessed exceptional imagination and superb smelting technology. In their surrounding mountains and rivers there were abundant metal reserves. They cast what they saw in real life as well as in their mind into bronze images, and then added a halo of divinity and altered the forms to express their idealism.

While people of the Shang Dynasty in the Yellow River Basin cast huge bronze vessels to symbolize power and holiness, their peers living on the wet and gloomy upper reaches of the Yangtze River cast vessels of similar technological challenge to express their preoccupation with nature and creatures.

The tiger-shaped gold foil unearthed at Sanxingdui

Moreover, people nowadays are more concerned with those mystified human figures that play leading roles in this world of bronze. In ancient Chinese civilization there are no other three-dimensional bronze human figures like them; their size is unparalleled in the Bronze Age throughout the world.

The unearthed bronze head sculpture with the gold face of Sanxingdui

The other discovery at the Sanxingdui ruins that was astounding were the gold objects whose sheer number, range of shape and volume were unmatched by any other discovery in Chinese archaeology at that time period.

Gold artefacts unearthed at Sanxingdui ruins are quite similar to the gold masks and sceptres buried in the tombs of Egyptian kings 3,000 B.C, the supreme representation of divine as well as earthly power in ancient Egypt.

Bizarre patterns on the gold staffs may also be religious symbols of some kind to emote or designate the presence of a divine power.

Gold masks make bronze statues even more solemn and noble. Researchers worldwide believe that early states emerged under the rule of individuals who were both political and religious leaders. At Sanxingdui, although the cultural origin is still unclear, those artefacts point to the existence of that kind of ancient civilization that began to voice its existence as a country or state in the upper reaches of the Yangtze River.

There used to be a huge kingdom here, dazzling, uproarious and wealthy. Their decisions were led by sorcery and their holy days were filled with sacrifices: they prepared sacrificial cattle, sheep, deer, elephants and human beings; gigantic bronze trees and bronze standing statues enjoyed their worship on tall altars. But who were these busy, solemn people? More accurately speaking, where did the ancient Shu people come from? What did they look like and how did such an advanced civilization meet its end and disappear for so many thousands of years?

Solved puzzles give rise to even more puzzles. Where were the altars that should have come together with sacrificial pits? Where were the city walls of the ancient kingdom? Archaeologists managed to restore artefacts unearthed in the 1986 excavation of the Sanxingdui ruins. People several thousand years before had broken or burned them into bits and pieces. Why had they destroyed those sacred objects before burying them so cursorily underground? What was happening at that time?

The evidence of their existence seems only to unravel the real mystery.

Chapter Seven
The Lost Kingdom

1934, a sketch of the Sanxingdui archaeological excavation, the site where the west wall of the ancient city was unearthed, was drawn by American anthropologist David Graham. Centered on the Yan compound, the site of his excavation, the sketch marked out important locations and the exact alignment of the ruins. In a sketch more than seventy years later, the boundaries and alignment are almost identical, except that three huge earthen ridges are now lying across the east, west and south sides of the Yan compound. These were the ancient city walls of Sanxingdui discovered by later archaeologists.

In 2005, while the excavation at the Qinglongbao ruins was going on, archaeologists unveiled another secret under the west wall of the ancient Sanxingdui city—the River Gate they had hypothesized.

Two water systems, the Yazi River and the Mamu River, are located to the north and in the center of the Sanxingdui ruins, respectively. In summers there is abundant water in the Yazi River. Geographically speaking, this area is crisscrossed by a dozen rivers belonging to either the Min River water system or upper reaches of the Tuo River water system. Since ancient times, the narrow Tuo River at one end of the Chengdu Plain, when flooded by several major

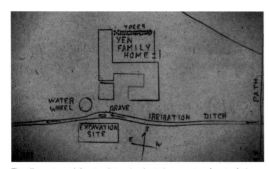

The illustration of Sanxingdui archeological excavation (portion) drawn by David Graham in 1934

American anthropologist David Graham (the first right in the below row) in Chengdu

Bronze birds unearthed at Sanxingdui

Cormorants in the Yazi River

tributaries in peak seasons, has frequently crushed the Jintang Gorge, blocking the entire waterway. Floods and storm water has earned the Chengdu Plain the bittersweet nickname of "West Sichuan; Where the Sky Leaks." Water plays a key role in civilization, but also gives rise to many stories of life and death over tens of millions of years.

Ancient images are still seen in the Yazi River close to the modernistic Sanxingdui Museum. Every summer, fishermen living nearby practice their trade in an extraordinary fashion. They use a water fowl to fish for them in the river. They call the hardworking cormorant birds "fishing crows", or "black ghosts" because of their characteristic raven black feathers and electrifying eyes.

Inside the museum, people see a lot of bronze birds with long beaks similar to that of a "black ghost". Why did they make such frequent appearances in the ancient kingdom of Sanxingdui? According to ancient records, the three earliest dynasties of Shu were Cancong, Baiguan and Yufu. Experts associate the image of these birds to Yufu. Nine birds perch on a bronze tree, all of them having long beaks similar to that of a "black ghost" and endued with a strong religious impression. On a gold staff, assumed to be the kingly sceptre, there are images of fish and birds too. Was Sanxingdui the capital of the Yufu Dynasty? Many researchers identify the literal meaning of Yufu in ancient records with the fishing "black ghosts" of today. Like Cancong's people, Yufu's tribe also lived in the Min River Basin and might probably be a branch of the former. At the very beginning they had fished and hunted on the part of Chengdu Plain that borders on the Min River, and then migrated further inland to fish in the numerous lakes and ponds there. Living in the pantheistic remote antiquity, they gradually elevated the fishing crow, something closely related to their life, to the status of a deity.

Most people comment that the images associated with the Sanxingdui kingdom are eerie. Since no remains of ancient inhabitants of Sanxingdui more than 3,000 years have been found, it is difficult even for experts to tell what they looked like. We come up with the likeness of Cancong and Yufu by referring to historical records, but how farfetched are they from reality?

The masks, with high-bridged noses, deep-set eyes and the part- human, part-divine being forms, prompt researchers and laymen alike to make all kinds of conjectures. Some link these images to Western Asia and Near East where they have found evidentiary support. Some others even regard these forms as likenesses of extraterrestrial beings.

Age-old sorcery is still performed in ethnic Qiang villages in the upper reaches of the Min River, where wizards bedecked with headdresses and masks chant scriptures. Their chants are actually the ethnic Qiang version of Creation in which scholars have found striking similarities with the historical accounts of ancient Shu.

According to historical annals Cancong's tribe originated from the Shu Mountains (today's Min Mountains). Annals penned in different time periods gave similar descriptions of Cancong and his tribe: they had cylindrical-shaped pupils which protruded from deep set eyes, lived in stone houses and got buried in stone coffins. An ancient ethnic Qiang epic, once translated, tells the tales of war between Geji aboriginals and ancient Qiang people arriving in the Min River Valley to settle. Geji aboriginals lived in stone houses scattered around the Ming Mountains and got buried in stone tombs. Defeated by white stones hurled at them by ethnic Qiang people, they were subdued and finally allowed the newcomers to settle, gradually being absorbed into the culture of the latter.

According to ancient literature and extensive research, the ancestors of Shu people were ancient Qiang people from the Qinghai-Tibet Plateau.

Before 1933 the ethnic Qiang people living here had been called "Cancong Qiang". Today many town

Old wizard of the Qiang ethic group

Young girls of the Qiang ethic group

dwellers still regard them as offspring of "Cancong Qiang". Beside the town there is a deep lake created by a major earthquake in 1933. An ancient city and many of its secrets are buried underwater.

The section of the Min River Basin between the river source and Chengdu Plain is mainly inhabited by ethnic Qiang people and Tibetans. They live much the same way as their ancestors. It could be safely said that modern archaeology may sometimes prove stories in history or stumble upon truth. In early 20th century, sure enough, stone coffins were discovered in the Min River Basin. Later excavations uncovered many more. In those coffins there are various potteries and bronze ware, as well as human remains arranged in some inexplicable posture. Is it the burial practice of Cancong's tribe as recorded in historical annals?

Still other puzzles remain about stones. In their epic, the Qiang people defeated enemies with white stones. Today their offspring still worship white stones. Can we find traces of ancient Shu people in stone houses inhabited by ethnic Qiang people today?

In ethnic Qiang villages in the Min River Basin, images related to bronze masks unearthed in Sanxingdui are seen everywhere. If the Sanxingdui bronze masks indeed drew inspiration here, then researchers will be able to prove another theory: the ancient Qiang nomads, a branch of Mongolians, roamed the Kunlun Mountains and Tianshan Mountains for a long period of time. Many ethnic groups from Western Asia, Central Asia and even Europe passed through and winded up congregating there over time. It was only after integration with other ethnic groups that ancient Qiang people dispersed across the Jinsha River, the Yalong River, the Bayankala Mountain Pass and the Min Mountains to become ancestors of modern ethnic Yi people, Tibetans and ethnic Qiang people. This might account for the distinctive features of these peoples today.

By 2005 archaeologists had discovered and unearthed ancient city walls on the east, west and south side of Sanxingdui, but not the northern one bordering on the Yazi River. Maybe the latter, as assumed by many people, has been washed away by floods in remote times. After years, excavated city halls and dwelling remains have marked out a city area of more than 3.5 square kilometers. The lost kingdom started to take on a more concrete shape.

Years later, people are still wondering: how could such a thriving kingdom be wiped out so suddenly? All kinds of conjectures have been made, from a dramatic power shuffle to the more poetic tale of war and death... However floods are the only cause supported by archaeological discoveries. If the ancient Sanxingdui kingdom was indeed destroyed by floods, then where did the people go?

Ancient literature has it that there were five reigns in the ancient Shu kingdom: the Cancong, Baiguan, Yufu, Duyu and Kaiming. Unlike the others, the Kaiming, as noted in annals, came from the middle reaches of the Yangtze River. The developments of all these dynasties were related to floods and flood control.

Stone coffins

Breakthroughs were made in the 20th century in research on the last dynasty of the ancient Shu kingdom, the reign of Kaiming, which was about the same time as the Spring and Autumn Period, or the Warring States Period. Much about it has been known with the 2000 excavation of unusual ship-shaped coffins containing royal family members of the Kaiming reign in downtown Chengdu.

Ship-shaped coffins containing royal family members of the Kaiming reign

However, experts find a lack of transition in both form and content between Sanxingdui artefacts and the Kaiming reign artefacts. They believe the missing link might be the fourth dynasty of the ancient Shu kingdom, the reign of the House of Duyu. Was it the blank to be filled in after the ancient Sanxingdui kingdom had been gone?

In spring 2001, an astounding discovery was made at a construction site in the outskirts of Chengdu some forty kilometers from the Sanxingdui ruins in Guanghan. Archaeologists from Chengdu Institute of Archaeology sped to the site. By and by a huge kingdom was exposed. The site was named Jinsha Ruins after the place where it is located. Objects unearthed at Jinsha ruins convinced the dazzled archaeologists that they could help explain what happened right after the vanishing of the ancient Sanxingdui kingdom.

Although weighing a ton in total, these unearthed objects were from just a tip of the entire site. Bronze human figures here have identical gestures with the bronze standing statues at Sanxingdui. Patterns on gold hatbands are very similar to those on the gold staffs of Sanxingdui, which are: fish, bird and man. Gold masks unearthed at Jinsha ruins share almost the same style with those found at Sanxingdui. The sun wheel of Sanxingdui was replaced by some other composition here, but both may embody the same spirit. The most important discovery, a piece of rectangular jade (*cong*) with round holes, has

The small standing bronze statues unearthed at Jinsha ruins

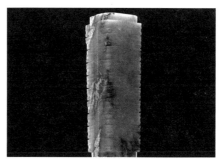
The rectangular sapphire blue jade with round holes unearthed at Jinsha ruins

The Sunbird Deity with gold foil unearthed at Jinsha ruins

Gold mask unearthed at Jinsha ruins

the distinctive style of Liangzhu Civilization in the lower reaches of the Yangtze River, which convinces us that even in ancient times the Yangtze River was a channel that helped civilizations spread and interact.

The way of life of ancient Qiang people has been preserved thanks to wizards who pass down epics from generation to generation by mouth. If answers were known as to why they stayed here, then the mystique around the Sanxingdui ruins may be lessened. If the upper reaches of the Yangtze River could be compared to the great river's childhood, then it is closer to obscuration and savagery, as well as the heavens and deities.

These sacred objects from ancient times are now worshipped in shrine-like museums. This is how posterity defines where they came from: the only civilization in the Yangtze River Basin three to four thousand years ago and an age that saw the peak of bronze technology. It was only several hundred years later those cities emerged on the middle and lower reaches of the Yangtze River.

These people were fleeing their homeland more than 3,000 years ago.

Bronze animal face unearthed at Jinsha ruins

Storms and floods had besieged their city. Sacred bronze vessels too cumbersome to carry away had been smashed and burned before getting buried hastily underground. When even greater floods descended upon the city, the people had gone.

A modern scholar said, "Without in-depth research of the ancient Shu civilization, we cannot have a complete picture of the origin and development of the Chinese civilization".

Chapter Eight
Chengdu, A City Nurtured by Water

Flower growers from suburban Chengdu were busy at the flower trading hall next to their village as early as four in the morning. Most of them used to grow crops, but as the need for flowers grows in the city, many have taken up growing fresh flowers for sale in the city center several kilometers away each morning.

It has been a long standing custom for Chengdu residents to drink a cup of morning tea while attending a storytelling session. Usually the story is about the most important part of history of this ancient city. The Emperor in the story is buried nearby in a grand mausoleum.

Every morning as storytellers at all teahouses in all alleys narrate the same story from history, Chengdu residents start their bustling morning.

When American Joseph Beech came here 100 years ago, he was so impressed by the leisurely air that hung over its rivers and people that he compared it to Eden in the Bible in his writings. In 1920 National Geography published his work The Eden of the Flowery Republic, in which he wrote about the tall firm city walls of Chengdu, its vast open country, and how the ancient

The storytellers

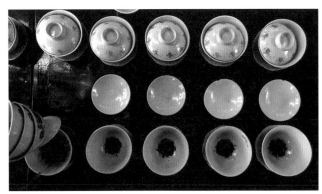

Chengdu Gaiwan Tea

Chengdu in dawn

capital was being quietly transformed by modern civilization.

Marco Polo, who had come to Chengdu even earlier, described his journey here, "This great river flows east towards the sea. It takes 100 days to travel the full length of it." According to him, there was a place called Chengdu on the plain where tributaries great or small converge to form a great river.

Chengdu was Eden in the eyes of Joseph Beech. In fact as early as 400 B.C. King Kaiming V of the Shu kingdom moved his capital here. Afterwards, despite vicissitudes, Chengdu has never changed its name. It is the only city in China that has managed to do so. Thanks to the superior natural environment and few wars, it has become a land of abundance in south-western China. Joseph Beech also attributed it all to the diligence and wisdom of local farmers.

"There are many rivers in Chengdu. Some girdle the city while others traverse it", Marco Polo's travel log noted. The rivers are still here, and in the care of present-day Chengdu people, they have become cleaner, greener and livelier.

Two man-tamed rivers girdle the city: the South (or Nan River), which is actually a split of the flow from the

The countryside at the west in Sichuan, by Beech in 1918

The rebuilt Funan Rivers

Min River; the second is Fu River. Emperor Xizong of the Tang Dynasty diverted what used to be called the Pi River to serve as a moat and renamed it the Fu. The river circles downtown Chengdu from the north as the South River coils around the southern and western parts. They run a course independent of each other for a total length of 17 kilometers before they meet and flow east into the Yangtze River, referred to as a "green necklace around the neck of Chengdu".

The history of the ancient city is intertwined with that of rivers. To generations of Chengdu residents, clear running water and active water traffic are integral part of their memory.

Marco Polo described the Anshun Bridge above the South River in his travel log, "Rivers from all directions either circle around or flow across the city. There is one bridge spanning one of the rivers, on whose floors are neatly arranged rooms and stores in all lines of business..."

The night scene of Anshun Bridge

Making the Sichuan brocade

The dough figuring in the Jinli Ancient Street

Record has it that in ancient Chengdu a great variety of merchandise was available; the most frequently traded one being a textile known as Sichuan brocade. Because of its well developed brocade industry Chengdu also goes by the name of Brocade City. Such brocade can only be rinsed in clean river water; therefore the South River was also called the Brocade River. Many years ago when people travelled up and down the river in boats they would see weaver girls rinsing brocade in the clear river water all around the city.

To Chengdu residents, it would seem that their old-fashioned hometown has taken on a fashionable new look almost overnight, in tune with the accompaniment of the murmuring water in the Fu and South Rivers.

Over 1,000 years ago cotton rose hibiscus were grown all over the top of Chengdu's city walls. Today there is a 17-kilometer green corridor along the Fu River and the South River. The legendary Eden is still one of the most eco-friendly cities in the world.

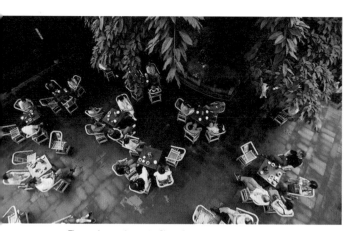
The outdoor teahouse in Chengdu

Teahouses in Chengdu may have best preserved tradition. Men and women, young and old, all gather here to chat over religiously prepared tea, as if it were some ceremony performed for the sake of rivers. In the 1950s Chengdu residents drew chilled river

The old Broad Alley

water to brew tea without bothering about filtration.

The process during which melted snow water from the Min Mountains makes its way to Chengdu could be a metaphor for man's progress from fighting against nature to living in harmony with it. Research shows that tea drinking started in Chengdu in the Warring States Period. The leisurely and carefree mood has never lifted throughout history. In this sense, a cup of tea tells all the secrets of Chengdu's prosperous and peaceful existence.

The age old Broad Alley in downtown Chengdu has gradually dilapidated, despite its long history as a well known, prime location. In recent years many old buildings in the area have been pulled down in the process of urban redevelopment. The government hopes to preserve the Broad Alley by demolishing some houses while restoring the others. Residents in the Alley know it as it is and wish that it could be left to age naturally.

Running water, fertile land and city walls turn Chengdu into a paradise for all. Monarchs, merchants and literati alike are attracted by its beauty and lifestyle. Almost all great poets in ancient China have been here. Today many poets, writers, painters and architects set up their studios on the outskirts of Chengdu.

Torrential snow water carried by the Min River meets a verdant mountain in the north-western Chengdu Plain. Between the river and the mountain are huge weirs, built in ancient times to tame the Min River before it rushed

Du Fu Thatched Cottage

Dujiangyan

further onto the Chengdu Plain. It is water that has endowed people living on this plain with wealth and an indescribably free attitude towards life. The weirs, although built more than 2,000 years ago, are still considered a world wonder in the history of water conservancy. Without these fascinating, innovative guardians, the Chengdu Plain wouldn't be what it is today.

The city of Dujiang Weirs got its name from the ancient weirs. On April 5th every year there is a grand ceremony in honor of Li Bing, chief architect of the Dujiang Weirs. On this day, farmers in western Sichuan can open the gates and draw off water from reservoirs to irrigate their fields.

More than 2,000 years after its construction, people still marvel at this water conservancy project the likes of which are not to be found anywhere in the world. What are its secrets of success?

Li Bing decided to build the weirs at a curve of the Min River because he could take advantage of the curve to induct river water into the main body of his project, which includes a bifurcation dam nicknamed the "Fish Mouth", Feisha Weir, and the Bottleneck. The bifurcation dam divides the river into two streams, the inner one for irrigation and the outer one for floodwater discharge. Feisha Weir, a floodway located in the middle, relieves flood while drastically reducing silt at the Bottleneck since whirlpools are formed as torrents rush into the outer stream. The Bottleneck, the in fall to the inner stream, controls the amount of water flowing into the plain.

More than 2,000 years after the completion of Dujiang Weirs, the Chengdu Plain has always been a fertile land where people farm, harvest and their families multiply.

Chengdu was one of the richest places on earth over 2,000 years ago thanks to rivers that carried its merchants and goods as far as the sea and back. Today Chengdu is still a city nurtured by water. Water continues to fill its happy memories and be its source of vitality.

Chapter Nine
Buddhism Extends Eastward from Here

At the foot of Lingyun Mountain where three rivers converge, there is an incredibly huge statue of Buddha. Upon first sight of the world's largest statue of Buddha carved out of an entire mountain, everyone exclaims in amazement about its gigantic size. It is tough climbing from the feet of the Buddha to the pate.

There is something special about this area in the upper reaches of the Yangtze River. Three rivers flow between the towering statue and an ancient city. It is here that the Qingyi River and the Dadu River empty into the Min River before the latter travels further east to become the largest tributary of the great Yangtze River.

To generations of residents of the ancient city, the huge statue of Buddha was a normal landmark, looking over their lives from the time they were born. They can't help wondering throughout their life why they had been favored so, that the largest statue of Buddha would materialize here and transform the mountain into its current shape. Even now curiosity over that same question is tempting many tourists to come here. On fine days people standing on top of Linyun Mountain can often see a peak faintly discernible in the distance. That is the famous Mount Emei.

Mount Emei is mysterious for its long history and seemingly

The Leshan Giant Buddha

The sea of clouds at Mount Emei

inexhaustible space, which is illustrated by a series of astounding data: over 1,600 medicinal plants that have similarities to those immortal herbs mentioned in mythology; more than 3,000 advanced flora and 2,300-plus fauna that make up this miraculous world; a peak that thrusts itself over 3,000 meters towards the sky from a gentle valley.

Mount Emei is made even more charming because of an age-old school of learning known today as "Buddhist philosophy", which, apart from the profound Sanskrit scriptures and ideals, also teaches people to follow realistic attitudes towards life that transcend time.

Over thousands of years people were converted and built palace-like temples all over the mountain. Legend has it that in the middle of the first century A.D. solitary Buddhist practitioners built Puguang Temple, the first temple in the Yangtze River Basin. Fuhu Temple (or Tiger Taming Temple), reportedly built in the late East Jin Dynasty, is now inhabited by nuns. In Buddhism nuns are called Bhiksuni.

Buddhism aims at replacing misery with beatitude for all people. Buddhist monks and nuns have focused on their own moral integrity since ancient times. Their pious life may seem mysterious to us, but in most ways they are not so different.

In remote antiquities the top of Mt. Emei might signify the highest

Religious ceremony on Mount Emei

The restored Golden Summit on Mt. Emei

attainment in religion to solitary forerunners. Therefore they aspired to practice Buddhism there where the sky seemed to be within reach. Earliest temples might have appeared on the top of the mountain, but records of them have been lost. More reliable information is found from the Ming Dynasty. During that time there were over 200 temples in the mountainous area, and on the summit there were a series of golden heavenly palaces, hence the name "Golden Summit". According to records, the huge expanse of summit temple flourished in the Ming Dynasty, the main attraction of which being a huge copper statue of Samantabhdra or Puxian (the Bodhisattva of Universal Benevolence).

On this summit more than 3,000 meters above sea level, one can't help being awed by the pristine snowy peaks in the distance and mountain ranges extending towards Mount Kunlun. However, the legendary golden temple is said to have been destroyed repeatedly by fires over hundreds of years.

In 2003, a cooperative preservation project between the Government and Buddhist practitioners rebuilt the long-gone temple and restored the sacred statue on the Golden Summit. Numerous modern materials and technology were used to reconstruct the grand landscape of the past. Surviving temples and statues of Buddha gave inspiration to restoration specialists. The new temple and statue were erected exactly where they were before.

There were other sources of inspiration in the restoration process: Buddhist pagodas inscribed with

Bhiksuni and the monkeys on the Mount Emei

The copper statue of Samamtabhdra or Puxian (the Bodhisattva of Universal Benevolence) at the Golden Summit of Mt. Emei

lengthy scriptures, scriptures written on mystic pattra leaves from India, a tooth relic of Buddha that is speckled like agate, and a 62-ton statue of Samantabhdra or Puxian cast over 1,000 years ago. Even now people can hardly imagine how this statue was cast and installed on the rugged Mount Emei.

In temples on Mount Emei, hundreds of monks and nuns perform ancient Buddhist ceremonies and preserve their traditional lifestyle. According to records in the peak times of Ming and Qing Dynasties, there were over 1,000 practitioners in the area.

Buddhism, which originated in India, spread to China in the first century A.D. via the northern and southern silk routes. The northern silk route stops short at Qinling Mountains, while the southern route links India, Burma, Yunnan Province of China, and the Jinsha River section of the upper reaches of the Yangtze River. Many people regard the latter as an important route for Buddhism to reach the Yangtze River Basin.

When did Buddhism spread to Leshan where three rivers converge? In the 1970s archaeologists excavated a cluster of East Han Dynasty cliff tombs 31 kilometers away from the giant

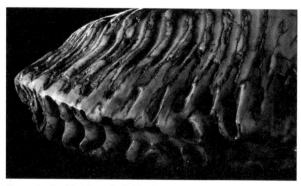

The tooth relic of Buddha at the Golden Summit of Mt. Emei

The Nirvana carving of Dazu Rock carvings

Buddha statue. There, apart from a great number of funerary objects, they also found images of Buddha in lotus position on tomb wall reliefs. The time when the cliff tombs were built coincides with the time believed by the academia when Buddhism spread to China. Time and place seem to fit perfectly. It is from here that Buddhism extends eastward throughout the Yangtze River Basin.

For years the actual origin of the Giant Buddha Statue had remained unknown. In 1982, researchers studied a stone tablet with barely legible inscriptions on a cliff face overhanging the river to the right of the giant Buddha statue. With efforts they gradually made out the writings on the tablet dating back to the Tang Dynasty, which turned out to chronicle the birth of the Giant Buddha Statue.

The tablet reads, "In the past floods pestered the Min River, killing people and livestock alike..." Haitong was a monk in a mountain temple where three rivers converged in the Tang Dynasty when Buddhism prevailed. According to the tablet it was Haitong's lifelong ambition to build an all-powerful giant Buddha statue on a riverside cliff to bring river devils to submission. After Haitong death, others picked up where he left off. It took more than ninety years to finish the statue.

The Dazu countryside

The Dazu rock carvings

For a long time the details of how and why the Giant Statue had been built were little known. Then by chance people found two pieces of hair bun fallen from the head of the stone Buddha. Made of giant stone slabs, the two pieces revealed the skill and life of ancient craftsmen. Upon further study people started to understand how the entire Giant Statue came into being.

To people's surprise the stone Buddha's hair bun was not carved out of one single rock. Instead, 1,021 stone slabs with shell patterns carved on them comprised the large section. The three drainage ditches hidden in between 18 distinct layers of hair bun are part of a ingenious drainage system that also includes secret passages behind the statue as well as lines on Buddha's gown. The seven-meter high ears and nose result from a precise wooden structure.

The Leshan Giant Buddha is also known to people as Maitreya, the future Buddha representing light and happiness. Images of Maitreya erected earlier than the one in Leshan seldom sit as squarely as the latter. Ancient people chose this posture to set squarely against the roaring torrents.

Still there are unresolved puzzles. The Giant Statue has managed to stand erect through ages because there isn't any apparent rupture zone where it is, thanks to far less drastic geological transformation. How did people living over 1,000 years ago realize the stability of this spot? Or was it simply a coincidence?

Few words were used in describing such a huge project, "Thousands of iron hammers rose and fell in the work field, and the big rocks tumbled to the ground with a sound like thunder." One day more than 1,200 years ago at the confluence of three rivers, craftsmen finally saw the result of their lifetime dedication soar into the clouds, but their name and life stories were soon washed away by the eastbound river water.

Nobody knows when such a practice started, but many farmers know how to carve statues of Buddha at Dazu County, Chongqing, hundreds of kilometers east of Leshan. More than 50,000 Buddhist rock carvings led a solitary existence for an extensive period of time in the wooded hills where farmers live. Hundreds of years later these gigantic but well-proportioned images astounded the world. Dazu is on the northern bank of the Yangtze River.

Between the Tang and the South Song Dynasties, Sichuan Province was seldom inflicted by wars. During this period of more than 1,000 years, travelling monks, craftsmen, merchants, and monarchs passed in and out of Sichuan via the Yangtze River and the paths along it. It was they who were the patrons who created the Buddhist wonderland at Dazu.

Time passed and the extensive winding grottoes of Dazu rock carvings faded into oblivion until Guo Xiangying arrived in the early 1970s. He was so fascinated by the rare rock carvings that he, without the aid of a camera or modern plotting technique, started to set up files for them by copying the Buddhist images one by one, one grotto after another.

The resulting 20-meter long scroll includes all important rock carvings and key grottos in Dazu's North Mountain and Baoding Mountain. About twenty years after the creation of the scroll, and the accompanying manuscripts of Guo Xiangying, these major documentations were brought to the forefront when the Dazu rock carving grottoes became a World Cultural Heritage site candidate.

The Dazu rock carvings entered the list of World Cultural Heritage sites in 1999. By then, Guo Xiangying was in his old age. In 1982, after prolonged efforts, he set up the Dazu Museum of Rock Carving Art. In the subsequent ten years or so during which he served as Director of the museum, the treasured rock carvings were subject to the systematic research and scientific preservation such World Cultural Heritage relics deserve.

Restored carving scene of Dazu rock carvings

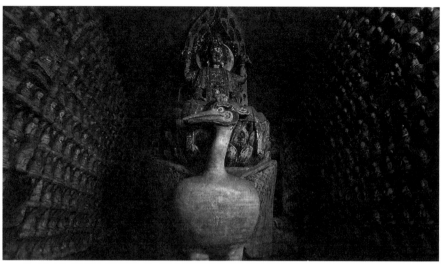

The north mountain grotto of Dazu rock carvings

Rock carvings in Grotto No. 136 of the North Mountain were masterpieces dating back to the North Song Dynasty. An exquisitely shaped prayer wheel supporting the grotto roof reminds people of the Buddhist concept of samsara. In the grotto, more than twenty Buddhist statues in the image of Chinese men and women are displayed.

The men were carved in bold strokes. The women look pretty, with a lot of details in clothing and shape, as if real blood were flowing beneath their smooth and fair skin.

The Thousand-Armed Goddess of Mercy (or Kwan-yin) and the Nirvana of Buddha nearby along a U-shaped stretch of cliffs in Baoding Mountain are solemn and imposing. There are many folktales about their creators in Dazu.

In 1159 Zhao Zhifeng, a 16-year-old Dazu monk set out on a study tour to western Sichuan. After studying under Liu Benzun, a Buddhist master, he

The Thousand-Armed Kwan-yin of Dazu rock carvings

came back to Dazu at the age of about 20 to start the rock carving project in Baoding Mountain. Liu Benzun himself was born in Leshan in 855 and closely related both in time and geography to the Giant Buddha Statue in Leshan. More than 100 years after the completion of the Giant Buddha Statue in Leshan, the last large-scale Buddhist

A series of Dazu rock carvings on parenting

rock carving project in Chinese history was launched in Dazu to its east.

Roughly 1,000 years later, Dazu people see the depictions of their daily life as well as the traditional Chinese values of loyalty, filial piety and sense of etiquette in those rock carvings.

There are a series of eleven groups of rock carvings on parenting, such as Praying for a Baby, Pregnancy, Delivery, Wedding, and Farewell, to illustrate how parents endure all kinds of hardships to raise their children and to exhort people to return parental love. They combine Buddhist teachings with Confucian ethics, the idealist philosophy of the Song and Ming Dynasties, and Taoism, providing a good case of Buddhism's adaptation to the Chinese culture.

In March 2006 the long-gone Giant Buddha Statue (Puxian) and temple were erected a second time on the sky-reaching Golden Summit of Mount Emei. Both their disappearance and reappearance sound like a myth. According to Buddhism the restoration done on the Gold Summit represents a most outstanding karma, which dates back to another age.

Today we are able to recapture the story of Buddhism and man in a short episode; whereas in the past 1,000 years or so it spread east as the Yangtze River surged east.

Chapter Ten
The Heaven-Blessed Chishui River

The Chishui River

Today many people are still wondering why the Chishui River is home to so many good liquors, the best among them, Maotai.

Record has it that people living in the Yangtze River Basin began to distil spirits as early as over 1,000 years ago. Some say it is the unusual sensation it gave the mind and the mysterious burning process that symbolized the transformation from yin to yang that earned liquor its important role in ancient sacrifices and ceremonies. It all started with the invention of distilling technology. Archaeologists have proven that the Taoist alchemists in the Yangtze River Basin who tried to make pills of immortality were the first in the world to invent distilling technology.

The Yangtze River originates from glaciers in the snowy Qinghai-Tibet Plateau and flows east, taking in tributaries on the way. When it arrives in Hejiang, Sichuan Province, another river from the Yunnan-Quizhou Plateau—the Chishui River–joins it. Before merging with the Yangtze, the Chishui River runs a full course of over 400 kilometers across Yunnan, Guizhou and Sichuan, starting from Zhenxiong, Yunnan Province. During the rainy season, the water in the Chishui River is colored red by deposits of eroded red soil that gather at its banks.

Along the middle reaches of the Chishui River and surrounded by mountains in Renhuai, Guizhou Province there is a small town known for

Maotai Town of Renhuai County, Guizhou Province

liquor making—Maotai. In 1915, some Maotai residents took their homemade liquor, took a boat onto the meandering the Chishui River, and then the Yangtze River, and then even further. At the Panama Pacific International Exposition held in the U.S that same year, the fragrance from a broken Maotai vessel won the hearts of wine and liquor tasters from around the world. Maotai was consequently awarded the gold prize that year. From that point after the long liquor distilling history of China as well as the obscure town of Maotai became world-famous.

Today the Yangtze River Basin boasts many famous spirits of China, but on its tributary the Chishui River liquors have become legends. 60% of the renowned liquor distilleries are scattered along the banks of the Chishui River. Go upstream from Hejiang County, Sichuan Province, and one finds a world of spirits. The Chishui River is also called "Good Liquor River" because of the many types of good liquor it helps produce.

Out of the rainy season, it takes on a different appearance: water so clear that fish swimming on its bottom can be seen; water so green that it sets off perfectly the reflections of red crops on river banks. The red crops are particular to liquor distilling here. The name is derived from the red soil they

The red crops

The restored scene of Yelang people making liquor.

are grown in and the red plump seeds.

In a village a dozen kilometers out of Maotai Town, farmers are busy harvesting the red crops. The formal name of those red crops is sorghum, one of the oldest crops in China.

Local farmers have been growing sorghum as a cash crop for generations. Today they are growing more and more of it for the well developed local distilling industry.

Why is this place so conducive to liquor making? Even locals don't know exactly. For many of them distilling is something they were born into.

Liquor burning

The age-old distilling practice in China makes use of such crops as sorghum, maize and sweet potatoes. The yeast is made from wheat. After fermentation and saccharification, the raw materials are boiled to extract their precious liquor. When the ethanol concentration reaches above 40% the liquor will start miraculously to burn,

Women treading on wheat mixture

a transformation from yin to yang, hence the name "burning liquor". Distilling techniques are easy to master for technicians today, but few of them could tell you when it all started.

Ancient records made note of the traditional and mysterious Maotai distilling practice. In olden times the yeast for Maotai was made by women treading on wheat mixture. The process was more like a ritual.

Such totem has been preserved. In today's Maotai Distillery only women are allowed in the yeast treading process. This step is so crucial to distilling that it is compared to a "Phoenix's Head" in midsummer when it takes place.

Why midsummer? Maotai Town's busiest time of the year is when all secrets unfold. All the vital procedures in Maotai-making are related to heat: yeast is prepared at high temperatures; fermentation is thrives at high temperatures; and the final distillation is completed at high temperatures.

Lest you think it only takes a summer, note the saying of the distillers, "It takes prayers; the patience of one who tries to comprehend the way of truth; and it takes all four seasons". High temperatures and a dialectical method of coinciding procedures with seasonal divisional points on the Chinese lunar calendar are crucial to Maotai making. There is the long cycle of stacking fermentation, tank fermentation, seven rounds of extraction, and nine rounds of boiling. No more can be explained because Maotai making techniques, confidential among locals for hundreds of years, were officially identified as a state secret in 1996.

On the west bank of the Chishui River workers at the Langjiu Distillery are working very hard as well. Like Maotai, Langjiu liquor is produced by yeast making, fermentation and distilling at high temperatures; and like Maotai, the exact production processes of Langjiu liquor are closely guarded secrets.

The natural liquor cellar

Liquor making is one of the ancient trades in China that has been passed on from generation to generation by oral instruction, rote memory and tacit learning. Despite the lack of written text, the heritage of these superb skills has survived over time. China has a long history of liquor distillation. Its spirits are divided into such different categories as "Fenjiu flavor", "Luzhou flavor", and "mixed flavor" on the basis of geography and history. The production of most Chinese liquors takes mere months without bothering about seasonal divisional points on the Chinese lunar calendar. On the other hand it takes a long time to make Maotai and Langjiu and there are stringent environmental parameters. The resulting Maotai flavor enabled Maotai liquor to become one of the world's three most famous liquors in as early as 1915, the other two being French cognac and Scotch whisky. Today, as the liquor served at state banquets, it embodies the Chinese spirit and temperament. Its strong,

The Maotai vessel in 1915

The golden medal the Panama Pacific International Exposition in 1915

long lasting zest stands for goodwill, sincerity, luck and happiness.

The Chinese character corresponding to "Maotai flavor", "Jiang", can be interpreted as "would-be liquor". Along the Chishui River this magic word not only encapsulates a unique evolution and a distinctive quality, but also predicates profound mystery. The "Jiang" flavor germinates on one particular

The Maotai workshop in the beginning of the 20th Century

seasonal divisional point on the Chinese lunar calendar and takes one full year, or all four seasons, to age. Seasonal divisional points are important in the Chinese tradition not only because they keep pace with nature, but also because they stand for ultimate completeness.

There are still various kinds of liquor stores in today's Maotai Town. However, recorded history of the town only goes back to the Qing Dynasty. People in Maotai want very much to know what it looked like in remote antiquity, and in the local museum they draw on imagination and legends to recreate it. At Maotai's State Liquor Museum a few sculptures and records are related to everyone's amazement, again to the Chinese character "Jiang". According to Historical Records, envoys of a West Han emperor found a good liquor made by the local "Lao" people living on the banks of the Chishui River. This liquor, which later became tribute liquor, was named "Gou Jiang". The same character Jiang was again used to depict the flavor of Maotai some 2,000 years later.

At the ancient Erlang Town, Gulin County of Sichuan Province, only a hundred miles away from areas inhabited by ethnic groups, many old people still claim that they are offspring of the "Lao" people. If true, this may actually tell

The changing procedure from the ancient liquor containers to the character "Jiang"

The ancient Erlang Town, Gulin County of Sichuan Province

a lot more about the history of the Good Liquor River. This ancient town once witnessed the most important chapter of the Chisui liquor making history. Some 400 years ago, the government enlarged the Chishui waterway between Hejiang, Sichuan Province and Erlang Shoal, Gulin to transport salt produced in Sichuan to Guizhou Province. Better access via the salt route gave an unprecedented boost to the age-old liquor business at Erlang and Maotai Towns.

The Chinese government has attached great importance to balancing ecological protection along the Chishui River with development of the Maotai liquor industry since the 1970s.

There is an old saying along the Chishui River which goes to the effect that water is the blood of liquor. Folktales related to water have been around for hundreds of years. Scientists find the geological formation here to be unique. Grit formed in the Jurassic Period and shale formed in the Cretaceous Period gave rise to the rare calcium-rich purple soil here. Groundwater and surface water were filtered by them before converging into clear, sweet and refreshing rivers and springs. Scientists also find a primeval ecosystem here, with the best preserved subtropical softwood forests throughout regions of similar latitudes, spinulose tree ferns dating back to the Jurassic Period, other rare flora and fauna, and a total of more than 3,000 biological species. The red clay that has a thickness between 500 and 900 meters is part of Danxia landform. Danxia rocks are conducive to bio-diversity and a balanced ecosystem because they

Nearly finished Maotai

help conserve water.

For years people living along the Chishui River have been musing over the many secrets underlying Maotai liquor. Theses and theories started to appear in the mid-1970s, but to this day only a few secrets have been disclosed. Researchers have identified a wonderland inhabited by omnipresent but invisible microorganisms. In different seasons there are different microorganisms, and they are most active in summer when there is high temperature and high humidity. It is mainly those summer that have earned Maotai flavor its legendary reputation, but the four seasons it takes to age Maotai liquor take advantage of them all.

Today's new generation of distillers know far more about those magical microorganisms than their predecessors. Originating from Yunnan Province, the Chishui River has been flowing at altitudes over 1,000 meters until it suddenly drops to a valley around Maotai Town only 400 meters above sea level. Mountains closing in on all sides isolate the area from the rest of the country. The Chishui River flows on the bottom of the long narrow valley, creating an environment of varied temperature, humidity and wind. This environment is ideal for the multiplication of microorganisms in the air, resulting in the best liquor from the full harvests of red sorghum crops, wheat and water.

As China's state liquor, Maotai has made a name for itself in the world with its unparalleled quality and profound history.

Chapter Eleven
Travelling on the Water

The Shiliupu Pier in Shanghai

In 2005 the volume of container transport at the Yangtze estuary ranked third in the world. Statistics in the same year showed that Yangtze River had the largest inland water cargo transport volume in the world. No matter how times change, the great river, with its inexhaustible energy, has always managed to bring people new wealth and new opportunities.

The Shiliupu Pier on the bank of the Huangpu River was built over 140 years ago. After witnessing the transformation of Shanghai from a small fishing village to a metropolis, it will be rebuilt into a world-class water tourism center in 2008.

To residents in Shanghai, the Shiliupu Pier is symbolic of the city's growth. More than 100 years ago, ships from inland and overseas anchored here, turning it into a hub for inbounding and outgoing cargoes. Trade attracted people to Shiliupu, making it the busiest port on the Yangtze River. Since then the Huangpu River has been known far and near. This river, which runs across Shanghai, is the last tributary of the Yangtze River before it rushes into the sea.

Chongqing is located upstream Yangtze River where the latter absorbs the Jialing River. More than 3,000 years ago, people disembarked at the confluence to settle. A town was gradually formed, which later developed into Chongqing. By and by the disembarkation point became the largest dock in the upper

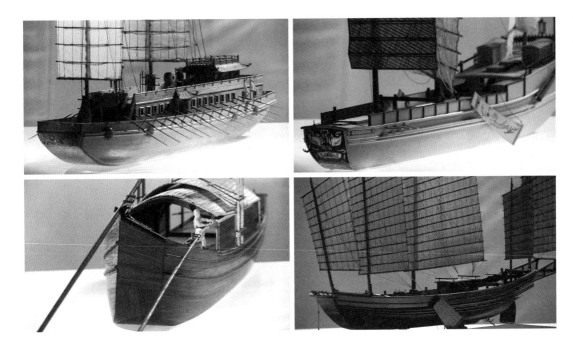

Ancient ship models collected by Jiaxin museum, Zhejiang Province. From above left to below right: the war ship on Yangtze River of the Three Kingdoms Period; ship for carrying grain in the Tang and Song Dynasties; the crooked-stern ship in the Ming and Qing Dynasties; the large junk of the Ming and Qing Dynasties.

reaches of the Yangtze River, Chaotianmen. For a long time this dock brought prosperity to Chongqing, and was known as the symbol of the mountain city. The 2,399-kilometer waterway between Chongqing and Shanghai is the major route for Yangtze River transportation.

With the exception of the Songliao Canal in north-eastern China, all other rivers in China's inland navigation network are connected to the Yangtze River mainstream at some point. This network extends in all directions for a total of more than 70,000 kilometers, 70% of the total mileage of China's inland water transport. This connectivity has also made the Yangtze River central to China's transportation and circulation of commodities. Articles of everyday use produced in Shanghai, steel manufactured in Wuhan, woollen textiles from Chongqing, as well as goods made in major cities along the Yangtze River, are moved across the country via the great river.

Although passenger transport on

The Shennong River in the Three Gorge of the Yangtze River

the Yangtze River seems to have peaked in the 1980s, ships were always able to cater to demands at different time periods. They carried soldiers in the Spring and Autumn Period, grains in the Qin and Han Dynasties, merchants and traders in the Tang and Song Dynasties, and added miscellany in the Ming and Qing Dynasties.

In thousands of years' time they helped economic contacts, cultural exchanges and racial integration and migration. About 100 years ago there were 170,000 wooden sailboats and some 200,000 plus boatmen. Thanks to cargo and passenger transport, political centers in northern China were able to be more closely linked to economic centers in the Yangtze River Basin.

In 1865 Xu Shou, a famous modern Chinese scientist, and his colleagues were busy at work at the Anqing Ordinance Factory on the bank of the Yangtze River. They were building China's first engine-powered boat. This wooden-hulled steamboat went by the name "Huanghu".

From then on engine-powered boats emitting dark smoke and man-powered boats and boats with big sails trudged side by side on the Yangtze River, something unique 100 years ago. At that time people were fascinated by the engine-powered boats which were about ten times as fast as those powered by wind or pushed on by hand along some stretches of the Yangtze.

In 1898, British captain Archibald John Little led a steamboat from Shanghai to the Chuan River upstream the Yangtze River. This voyage was more like an adventure since the terrifying Chuan River had been off limits to engine-powered boats. After running up on rocks and getting stranded, the boat was well riddled with gaping holes. Having finally made it to Chongqing, it was a strange sight to the wooden sailboats on the Chuan River.

The last city along the Yangtze River to be accessed by engine-powered boats, Chongqing benefited from the latter as well. Compared with traditional boats on the Yangtze River, engine-powered boats fared much better in speed and carrying capacity.

The freight ship "Min Sheng" on the Yangtze River in 1923

They helped attract business and people alike to docks alongside the Yangtze River, and in turn the cities around those docks became the first batch of big modern cities in China.

Today's freight ship "Min Sheng"

The freight ship Min Sheng calls regularly at Chongqing's Chaotianmen Dock. It reminds older Chongqing residents of the past. The two Chinese characters "Min Sheng" have been written into the city's history. In 1926 the first ever engine-powered passenger liner travelling on the Chuan River was named "Min Sheng" too. This ship was the first ship owned by Lu Zuofu, who later became known as the shipping tycoon of the Yangtze River. It was the "Min Sheng" ship and the Min Sheng Shipping Company that launched the tycoon into a legendary career.

When the War of Resistance against Japanese Aggression broke out in 1937, all Chinese ships on the Yangtze River were commandeered to evacuate materials and people from the war zone to the relatively safe rear. Lu Zuofu and his fleet played a major role in this strategic evacuation, carrying the hope of Chinese national industry to the area around Chongqing. This strategic move showed the Chinese determination to fight against the Japanese till the end. The solemn and heroic mission lasted several years. After the war, the Min Sheng, which was bombed down by Japanese aircraft, still lives on in people's memory. It is likened to a vital spark that gets rekindled in every ship on the Yangtze River. The present-day freight ship Min Sheng is the largest ship travelling up and down the Chuan River. This 1,500-ton roll-on roll-off ship is able to send a full load of motor vehicles from Chaotianmen to other cities along the Yangtze River. Geographical conditions limit the navigability of different sections of the river. On mainstream Yangtze River a 1,500-ton ship can reach Chongqing, a 5,000-ton ship can reach Yichang, while a 10,000-ton ship can travel between Nanjing and the river mouth. So many giant hauls come and go everyday; hence the reputation "Golden Waterway".

Navigation Light No. 1 on the Yangtze River is positioned where the Yangtze

The Paotaiwan dock at the Yangtze River estuary

River joins the sea. This is the starting point for ships to enter the Yangtze River. Any foreign ship will have to wait until a licensed Chinese pilot is on board.

It is the pilot's task to give directions to ships so that they can enter and exit safely. According to international norm, piloting, which stands for national sovereignty, is compulsory for all foreign ships coming in and going out of a harbor.

On November 19th 1982, the 25th Meeting of the Chinese People's Congress decided to "open the ports of Nantong and Zhangjiagang to foreign ships." On May 7th 1983 Japan Trader, a freight ship registered in Panama carrying 11,024 tons of timber, arrived safely at Berth No. 1 of Zhangjiagang under the guidance of one of the first Chinese pilots on the Yangtze River. Since then many foreign ships have travelled up the Yangtze River.

An epoch-making standard was created in cargo transport in the 1950s. A rectangular box, or a container, became the standard unit of world logistics. These standardized containers contain input factors from all over the world. For a country, the number of containers it handles measures how developed its manufacturing industry is. When the Chinese economy started to take off more than twenty years ago, freight ships on the Yangtze River, Chinese and foreign alike started to carry containers.

A beacon built by the Dutch over 100 years ago marks out Wusongkou, where the Yangtze River and the Huangpu River converge. In 1992, a huge floating dock, the largest in China, was completed beside the solitary beacon. Known as Paotaiwan Base, this dock relieved the Shiliupu Dock, an already busy dock that became overwhelmed when foreign ships were allowed in as well, of some traffic. In contrast to Shiliupu, Paotaiwan is more suitable for transit shipment. This huge breakwater-like base connects the Yangtze River and the Huangpu River. Here, arriving boats are reorganized into fleets, and cargoes are consigned onto bigger ships. Afterwards they are allowed to go on the next

Shanghai Waigaoqiao Container Terminal

leg of their journey.

The Yangtze River estuary is a dozen sea miles away from Paotaiwan, where the 6,380-kilometer long river fans out to empty into the sea at a much more leisurely pace. Known as the Bell, this water area is the greatest bottleneck of the Yangtze River fairway. Millions of tons of sand are carried by the Yangtze River and eventually deposited here. As a result, the fairway is always too silted up for large vessels.

On January 27th 1998 all kinds of engineering ships gathered at the Yangtze River estuary to participate in China's largest water transport project, the Yangtze River Estuary Deep Water Fairway Project. Three generations of experts and forty years' study later, a way to transform the Yangtze River estuary fairway was finally identified. A 50-kilometer long semi-spherical hollow dyke was laid on top of specially treated sea bed, blocking sediments from the fairway. This is indeed the Great Wall on the sea. Thanks to this innovation, the fairway at the Yangtze River estuary is now as deep as ten meters, adequate for 100,000-ton container ships. In the near future, when the water depth reaches 12.5 meters, even 200,000-ton container ships will be able to travel up the Yangtze River.

Of all container terminals, the Shanghai Waigaoqiao Phase IV Container Terminal is the one closest to the Yangtze River estuary. Every week thirty-

The sand-preventing dyke of waterway at Yangtze River Estuary

The Huangpu River at night

seven scheduled container ships from thirteen international shipping companies arrive from overseas to unload here. Afterwards the containers will be forwarded to ports along the Yangtze River. According to some statistics the Yangtze River carries as much as twenty times the freight of the Beijing-Guangzhou Railway. Convenient water transportation has helped turn the Yangtze River Basin into the manufacturing center for China or even the world. Today, as more container terminals are built in major cities along the Yangtze River, their neighbors, the passenger terminals, are less and less patronized.

Rapid development of alternative means of transportation in the past decade has changed people's preferences. A passenger ship on the Yangtze River that used to carry more than 1,000 people now carries only a dozen. Meanwhile cargo transport on the river has never been as active.

On October 31st 2001 all passenger ships on the middle and lower reaches of the Yangtze River were decommissioned. It was the last day of active service on the river for many captains.

At night the Huangpu River is lit up. Tourists are enjoying the beautiful sceneries on both banks as they cruise along the river. The former captain of Dong Fang Hong has got a new job, captain of Captain II. On each trip Captain II carries over 100 passengers to cruise about two kilometers on the Huangpu River.

One day in 2005, the luxury cruise Shenzhou owned by China Changjiang National Shipping (Group) Corporation arrived at the Three Gorges Ship Lock after having left Shanghai ten days before. Once through the spectacular Three Gorges Dam, Shenzhou took tourists from all over the world to the enchanting Three Gorges. Unlike the tourists two decades before, these passengers were able to take in the latest development along the banks, and could go much further into the Three Gorges.

The Mighty Yangtze

Chapter Twelve
A Mountain City of Water and Fire

Nowadays speed is paramount; it is in the blood of Chongqing residents. One could well say that their rapid-fire speech and prompt tendencies to take action are leftovers from the days when their ancestors had to fight for their survival against threatening mountains and roaring currents.

The night of Chongqing

After it became the fourth municipality under the direct jurisdiction of the central government in 1997, Chongqing began transforming at an incredible pace. Eight years later, its urban area is expanding at a rate of twenty-five square kilometers every year, and the number of non-agriculturally employed population is growing by some 400,000 to 600,000 every year. At present, Chongqing is 2.4 times the total area of the other three municipalities under the direct jurisdiction of the central government. Maps of Chongqing have to be updated every three months.

Two ancient rivers have been silent witnesses to the city's growth and expansion. Sheltered in a valley and saddled by the Yangtze and Jialing Rivers, Chongqing has an unusually hot climate owing to the endless mountain ranges that stretch from its west to its east. Meteorologists nicknamed it a "Stove" or a "Heat Island". Since ancient times, the valley's rapid currents and heated environment have produced notably courageous and uprightness Chongqing locals. The unique environment determines the character of this city and its people: strong, valiant, fast and resilient. This is a city of fire and water.

The Yuzhong peninsula in Chongqing

Downtown Chongqing, which was built around a monument, is now crowded with all kinds of modern buildings. Like any other modern metropolis, it is bustling with business, filled with prosperous and fashionable people. The monument, known today as the Liberation Monument, used to have another name in days when the city played the role of an iron-willed hero ready to sacrifice itself: Mental Fortress. In the 1930s and 1940s, Chongqing, despite its inland location in south-western China, was bombarded by the cruellest air strikes in history. Yet fate destined it to become the interim capital of China in the War of Resistance against Japanese Aggression. People erected this monument in between air raids to demonstrate their confidence and determination. Throughout the war the monument encouraged all Chinese to live and fight.

Lu Zuofu, a Chongqing native, made a name for himself in wartime Chongqing. Between 1939 and 1942, the fleet of ships owned by his family braved scrapes with Japanese bombers to transport materials and people through the Three Gorges to the wartime capital. New blood was injected into the city at the expense of almost all the existing ships at his Min Sheng Shipping Company. Starting from 1937, almost all political, economic and cultural institutes were relocated to Chongqing, triggering the thousand-year-old city to sprawl out of the peninsula along both banks of the Yangtze River.

Unique geography plus tenacity enabled Chongqing to survive the eight-

Fashionable lady of Chongqing

Chongqing is famous for its beautiful ladies

The Chongqing Liberation Monument in 1942, 1983, 2006 (from left to right)

year War of Resistance against Japanese Aggression and rise anew from the rubble.

The city was built more than 3,000 years ago by warriors and soldiers from the middle reaches of the Yangtze River. Due to the difficulty of land access and the known reputation for its valiant residents, Chongqing has survived against all odds. More than sixty years ago, the Japanese air force dropped bombs onto this mist-enveloped city which they could hardly reach on land.

In 1982 all aspects of Chongqing were recorded systematically on colored film for the first time in history. In the movie people see this heroic city, a pocket of thriving life enclosed by mountains; all the streets, roads and houses seeming to have grown miraculously out of hard rocks, age-old mist hanging in the air, and people carrying the same looks and postures inherited from ancestors.

Hotpot, a choice food originating from Chongqing, is famous for its spicy, hot, and scalding taste. At first people didn't consider pork and beef eaten with hot peppers, Chinese prickly ash seeds, ginger, garlic and butter a delicacy. It was just food for rough torrent-fighting boatmen and helmsmen. Local history, geography or the temperament of Chongqing natives may have all been conducive to the enduring popularity of hotpot. Today hotpot has become a significant cuisine of its own.

Less than ten kilometers from the Ciqikou Dock on the Jialing River is the site of the famous Chaotianmen Dock in olden days. It is here that the Jialing River joins the Yangtze River, and it is

Chongqing hotpot

The Ciqikou Ancient street in Chongqing

also here that the first Chongqing hotpot was served. Since ancient times the Chaotianmen Dock, where ships and merchants came and go in an endless stream, has been the busiest of all seventeen city gates along the river. As a landmark of Chongqing, it was also devastated by Japanese air strikes during the War of Resistance against Japanese Aggression.

In July 2005, a symbolic ancient building at Chaotianmen, the Hunan and Hubei Guild Hall, was being restored. Some say it was Gods' blessing that it survived the Japanese carpet bombing. Built by immigrants and merchants from Hunan and Hubei, the Hall contained wood engravings depicting their arrival here. Immigrants always gathered here between the Qing Dynasty and the War of Resistance against the Japanese Aggression. It is proof to the fact that Chongqing has long been a city of immigrants.

To a certain extent the two rivers together with the surrounding mountains have had more impact on the tenacity of Chongqing residents, producing in them a strong will and peremptory air. The extraordinary hardiness demonstrated during the Anti-Japanese War was not an anomaly. During an ancient war that was chronicled in warfare history books, Chongqing residents held their ground in a siege that lasted 36 years. In the 1980s, people in Chongqing were still leading their life in the old way—bustling, intimate and kind despite the mobilizing forces of change that brought rebirth to their city almost overnight.

The fact is that since the 1950s Chongqing has been gradually transformed from a military and political center in eastern Sichuan to an economic center in the upper reaches of the Yangtze River. Thanks to foundations well laid in the Anti-Japanese War years and right after the establishment of the People's Republic of China, the industrial sector grew rapidly into the mainstay of Chongqing's economy. In the 1980s, its geographical location right between the more developed East and the resource-rich West made it all the more important.

Chongqing was opened to foreign trade at the end of the 19th century. Influence of Western culture spread here via the Chuan River more than 100 years ago. At that time most Western clubhouses were built on the southern bank of the Yangtze River, echoing the ancient dock and guild halls across the riverbank. One example of leftover Western architecture preserved at one end of Riverside Avenue south of the Yangtze River has been turned into a romantic bar, from whose balcony one can see Chaotianmen, Chongqing's oldest dock, across the river. Lights twinkle along the bank, as does their reflection in the eastbound river.

Dragon lantern making has been with farmers in rural Tongliang County, Chongqing, for over 1,000 years. Dragon lantern dances are usually performed at important holidays and events in Chongqing to the accompaniment of splashing molten iron, hence the name "fiery dragons". The longest dragon lantern in people's memory was the 50-plus-meter one made in 1997; it danced in celebration with the strong, upright people of Chongqing when it became a municipality under the direct jurisdiction of the central government.

The Huguang Guild Hall is under restoring.

The Chaotianmen Dock in Chongqing

Chapter Thirteen
The Witness of Three Gorges

Archaeological expeditions in the Three Gorges area proved that the ancient civilization was closely related to that of the Chinese civilization. Ages ago, people regarded this area as a place of savagery and barbarism, but now no one doubts that civilization here was well developed in the Tang, Song and Ming Dynasties.

On June 8th 2003, the water level at the Three Gorges rose abruptly by more than 100 meters, enabling archaeologists to climb the sheer cliff faces of the Xiling Gorge and study the mysterious cliff tombs of ancient people. To their surprise, there were a dozen bronze weapons lying about three skeletons. Scientific tests dated them at 2,500 years old. All else about these remains is still unknown.

Archaeological discoveries at the Tactics Book and Sword Gorge spanned such a long time that people are now overwhelmed more by the mystique of the Three Gorges than the spectacular view. The Three Gorges Project, which started in 1993, submerged an area of more than 60 kilometers extending from the east to the west of the Three Gorges. Answers to many

The archeological team was excavating the cliff tombs of ancient people of the Three Gorges.

The bronze Chunyu (a kind of musical instrument) of the Warring States Period collected by the Three Gorges Museum

anthropological questions as well as invaluable heritage from ancient inhabitants of the Three Gorges might be buried right under land that is to be inundated soon.

The planned construction period for the Three Gorges Project is from 1993 to 2009. Having so much to salvage as the clock ticks away, Chinese preservationists of cultural relics are faced with two probable outcomes: working wonders or getting gripped by guilty conscience whenever the idea of posterity pops up.

In Chinese history bronze ware stands for an age of killing and bloodshed as well as glory. The huge number of unique bronze ware brings us closer to an obscure nation that seems to have an uncommon history.

The Pengxi River empties into the Yangtze River. Phase II of the Three Gorges Project will submerge the entire Pengxi River Basin. Mysterious tombs are scattered along the lower reaches of the Pengxi River where it joins the Yangtze.

People are very familiar with those legendary old buildings on both banks

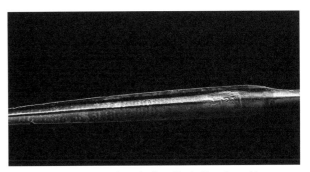

The Ba-style willow leaf shaped sword collected by the Three Gorges Museum

The excavation site in Yujiaba, Kai County

of the Three Gorges for the history and culture they reflect. Today they are more valuable because of their distinctive architectural styles and the steles inscribed by generations of literati.

Cultural relics to be inundated by the Three Gorges Reservoir are major targets of salvage digs and grounds relocation projects. Those precious images have become part of history. When relocating temples and other buildings, each brick or tile is carefully numbered so that on the new site they can be put back in exactly the same order. It is far tougher relocating them in exact detail than building them in the first place. Ancient inscriptions on cliff faces are cut and removed in their entirety. Although the technique has been adopted in the preservation of Egyptian cultural relics, preservationists find applying it under the unique geological conditions at the Three Gorges a different challenge.

The other method of preservation is to erect dams or walls to protect the hills on which the cultural relics stand as well as the surrounding vegetation. June 2003 was a gratifying month to Chinese preservationists, because the whole world bore witness to the rebirth of those wonders above the Phase I water level of the Three Gorges Reservoir.

The Wen Family Compound, built in the late Ming Dynasty and early Qing Dynasty, is a quadrangle of two rows of houses covering an area of more than 300 square meters. It is a traditional Huizhou-style architecture built mainly from brick and timber, but there are also traces of the post-and-tie style particular to the Three Gorges area. The entire compound is richly decorated and individual houses interlock with each other at their corners. The Wen family tree shows that the family moved here eleven generations ago, but it remains unknown where they moved from.

Dachang is to be submerged by Phase II of the Three Gorges Project. This ancient town, including the Wen Family Compound, is the top priority in cultural relic grounds relocation.

Over 6,000 square meters of ancient buildings and cultural relics at Dachang will be relocated, including 30 houses, two temples, and three sections of city walls together with gates. According to the relocation plan, all bricks, tiles, pillars and beams must be restored exactly as they were.

Dachang is to be relocated to the bank of yet another river, the Daning River, more than 30 kilometers away. In order to recreate the natural environment of the ancient town, an immense hill is being razed to the ground.

The Daning River is the largest tributary of the Yangtze River in the Three Gorges area. Archaeologists have long been concerned with flatlands along tributaries of the Yangtze River. Excavation at Dachang has been going on since 1994. So far much has been unearthed, though little is known of the ancient inhabitants who settled here over 3,000 years ago.

The Daning River joins the Yangtze River at the Wu Gorge of the Three Gorges. Archaeologists believe that inhabitants of the Dachang valley thousands of years ago entered the valley via the Wu Gorge.

A gigantic museum is under construction in downtown Chongqing to provide permanent accommodation to cultural relics found in the Three Gorges area throughout the years of this phenomenal project.

This museum, born in the backdrop of the Three Gorges Project and the daunting cultural relics salvaging task, is unconventionally large. It is named the China Three Gorges Museum. Receiving the largest impact in the process of Three Gorges cultural relic's

The dome of the Three Gorges Museum

The five-people tomb of the Neolithic Age in the Three Gorges

excavation and preservation, Chongqing has a good opportunity to sort out its long history. Historical records show that Chongqing was built by the Ba people from the Three Gorges area more than 3,000 years ago. Today Ba is another name for Chongqing, but little is known about the Ba people.

Archaeological discoveries have proven the existence in remote antiquity of highly civilized Chu and Shu peoples on the plains on either side of the Three Gorges, but the long narrow valleys in between have seldom been explored. The Three Gorges archaeological study gets us closer to a nation in history, the Ba people. Long ago the Ba people created the Ba & Chu Cultures when they adventured east and the Ba & Shu Cultures as they moved inland. Afterwards geographical advantages enjoyed by the Three Gorges made it a key link in the extension of the Chinese civilization in all four directions.

The earliest remains of the Ba people have been linked to the Daxi Culture discovered at the Qutang Gorge. The rich vestiges of the Daxi Culture point to refined life 5,000 years ago. This landmark culture of the Neolithic Age in China emerged right in a gorge of high winds and rapid currents. It would have been unimaginable that, thousands of years later, when the water level at the Three Gorges rose to a historical

The Ba-style bronze kettle inlaying silver of the Warring States Period collected by the Three Gorges Museum

The schematic map of the Baiheliang Underwater Museum

The Baiheliang stone fish

high, the life of ancient gorge inhabitants would be revealed and their daily utensils found. Those mysterious utensils have travelled across time to give us a glimpse to the life of their owners in remote antiquity. With them the past of the Three Gorges civilization was no longer an abstract concept.

In March 2005, coordinators working on the underwater project to preserve the Baiheliang (White Crane Ridge) Epigraph were in the middle of a meeting. It is the most challenging task among all salvaging projects at the Three Gorges. Eventually a decision was made to build a museum forty meters under water.

Normally the Epigraph emerged from water in its entirety every three to five years during the Yangtze River's dry season. On a ridge more than 1,000 meters long were stone fish and crane carvings for measuring water levels dating back to the Tang and Song Dynasties, as well as inscriptions of literary works related to hydrology. Recording hydrological data of seventy-two dry

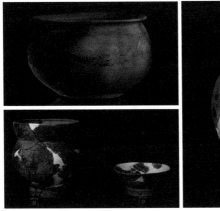

The painted pottery of the Neolithic Age collected by the Three Gorges Museum

seasons of the Yangtze River, it is by far the earliest and largest low-water mark hydrological epigraph in the world.

The preservation project derives its urgency from the cruel fact that the Epigraph will never see the daylight after the completion of the Three Gorges Reservoir and eventually get buried forever in silt some three decades years later.

This is the world's first under water museum built at such a depth. Many years later, people will be still able to travel back in time under the dreamy currents of the Yangtze River.

At present, the Chongqing Museum is a huge treasury home to 300,000 pieces of cultural relics that used to lie in oblivion under earth in the Three Gorges area. For visitors it is strangely fantastic to feel and touch them. Several thousand years of civilization in the Three Gorges area are encapsulated here. Those beautifully painted pottery are now on exhibition at the museum together with their owners to illustrate a special era in the Chinese civilization, the Neolithic Age.

Bronze ware excavated in the Three Gorges area spanned the entire

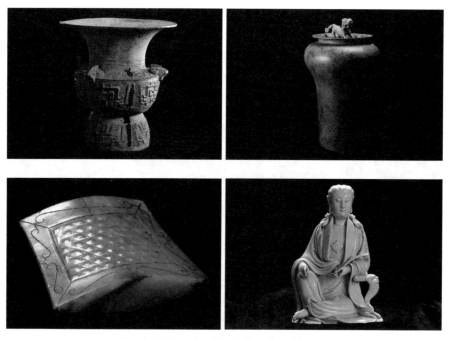

The cultural relics collected by the Three Gorges Museum

The restored Ba people head sculpture

Chinese bronze civilization from the Shang Dynasty more than 3,000 years ago through the Warring States Period, the Qin and Han Dynasties. Their craftsmanship and social attributes are on par with their peers found in the Central Plains, which means that like the Central Plains, this area has seen both elegant life and bloody warfare.

Exquisite jade ornaments the same age as the bronze ware emanate a smooth serene sheen that immediately captures the heart of museum goers.

More than 100 ruins and tombs of the Ba people were discovered in the Three Gorges archaeological study. However, since the remains in tombs have almost completely decayed, we could only conjecture what these mysterious people looked like from the bronze ware. The few skeletons that were still intact were found at the Qing River near the Xiling Gorge. From these samples, restoration experts reconstructed the image of the Ba people over 3,000 years ago. We finally have a better idea of the image of the ancient people in the Three Gorges area as well as their life.

In a valley up the Daning River dozens of miles away from Dachang some ancient hanging coffins are still perched on precipitous cliffs, reminding us of the profound mystery and long history of the Three Gorges.

The restored picture of the Ba people's fighting scene in the war

Chapter Fourteen
The Dam,
A Long Cherished Dream

The wind was freezing on January 3rd 1981, the day when the mighty Yangtze River was blocked for the first time in history. People arrived early in the morning to witness the grand occasion at the Gezhouba Dam construction site outside the Nanjin Pass of the Three Gorges. Few of them would realize that this dam was only prelude to a grander symphony.

Twenty years later, ships were able to pass the Gezhouba Dam and navigate the Xiling Gorge, the middle section of the Three Gorges notorious for its dangerous shoals and sinister rocks. Another magnificent project to tame the eternal river was conceptualized.

This is the world's largest water conservancy works. The completion of the Gezhouba Dam, the First Dam on the Yangtze River, more than twenty years ago foreshadowed this unrivalled project. It proved that the Chinese engineers and construction teams have sufficient technological capabilities to undertake an even greater project.

Today the over 2,000-meter long dam at the Three Gorges has been completed. With its erection, the great river has experienced some unprecedented changes.

People arrived early in the morning to witness the grand occasion of the Yangtze River being blocked.

An aerial view of the Three Gorges Dam

In summer 2004, a severe rainstorm suddenly befell the upper reaches of the Yangtze River. The continuous rainfall pushed up the water levels at the strategically important Jingjiang section to the warning line.

The Huangling Temple is located four kilometers downstream from the Three Gorges Dam. A flood in 1870 turned the Hubei and Hunan Plain into a vast expanse of water covering over 30,000 square kilometers and drowning millions of people. The water level of the Yangtze River rose to 81 meters in front of the Huangling Temple, a dozen meters higher than it was during the devastating flood in 1998. The flood rushed into the Huangling Temple and reached the top of the four-meter tall statue of Dayu.

Dayu, the water control hero worshipped by the Chinese, was so preoccupied with his work that he didn't get inside his house although he was literally on its doorsteps three times in a row. Hanging above his statue in the temple is a tablet whose inscription reads, "Digging through Rocks to Tame the Water", a reflection of the ancient Chinese aspiration to bring floods under control. However, in the summer of 1870, "Digging through Rocks to Tame the Water" seemed to be a goal beyond reach.

To people's amazement, the 1870 flood left marks on the sixteen pillars at the Hall of Dayu of the Huangling Temple. Those marks became important hydrological data for the Three Gorges project more than 130 years later.

In several thousand years' time the Chinese living along the Yangtze River have experienced hundreds of floods, big and small. Water conservancy experts estimate that after the completion of the Three Gorges project, the reservoir could be emptied

The ancient Huangling Temple

The water-wheeled electricity-generating units of the Three Gorges Project

before the flood season and get ready to receive more than 20 billion cubic meters' flood water to mitigate the threat to the lower reaches of the Yangtze River. The flood water would not be discharged until after the flood peaked.

Crisis was imminent. The flood diversion mechanism of the Three Gorges project was activated. In the turn of a hand something extraordinary happened: the raging torrents in the Yangtze River suddenly quieted down, and the flood was reined in at the foot of the dam. Within few days, the water level in the reservoir rose gradually by 1.2 meters from the original 135 meters.

A mere rise of 1.2 meters actually means that a total of over half billion cubic meters' flood water was held back and stored.

Several days later, when the flood peak in the lower reaches had weakened enough, more than twenty sluice gates of the Three Gorges Dam were opened to release the over half billion cubic meters of flood water. The half billion will be dwarfed by the flood control capacity of over twenty billion cubic meters upon completion of the Three Gorges reservoir. However, the statue of Dayu at the Huangling Temple as well as tens of millions of people living on the middle and lower reaches of the Yangtze River might have already been spared from drowning from that night to this day.

The statue of Dayu in the Huangling Temple

It is an enormous project to build a dam across such a great river. Foreign experts once claimed that it would be "a question bank for the world's hydropower industry". Technological challenges in this project are all unique in the world history of water conservancy project construction.

The construction site of Three Gorges Dam   The armature assembled by a stack of steel pieces

More than 100,000 design drawings spanning 40 years are now sealed up for safekeeping at the archive of the Changjiang (or Yangtze River) Water Resources Commission. Wordless as they are, these drawings are pivotal in realizing the Chinese dream of "a smooth lake rising in the narrow gorges".

Viewed from above the Three Gorges Reservoir resembles a huge water vessel hemmed in by mountains. The dam stands at a gully downstream. Twenty-eight million tons of concrete were poured to create the dam, more than two times the amount consumed by the Itaipu Hydropower Station in Brazil, at present the largest in the world.

Clear snow water from Gela Dandong rushes 5,000 kilometers to feed the gigantic 700-megawatt power generation units at the Three Gorges project. Water power that has been wasted for thousands of years is now finally being converted into electricity.

With twenty-six 700-megawatt turbine and generator units, the Three Gorges Power Station can generate 6.5 times the electricity as the Gezhouba Hydropower Station, an annual savings of 50 million tons of coal from coal-fired power plants. Today, as China is concerned with worldwide energy crises and power shortages, the power generated by the Three Gorges project is indeed good news. Clean and renewable, it will light up half of China.

The vast and mighty river surges eastward. During the past century several generations of Chinese people devoted themselves heart and soul to the Three Gorges project, a great project in the most poetic canyon in China. Today, the lofty Three Gorges Dam has already become the most striking landmark built in the past twenty years. It will have to stand the test of time and nature to keep its revered place.

With the completion of the Three Gorges Dam, this challenger for the title of "largest dam and hydropower station in the world" will find its way into geographical and engineering literature around the world.

Chapter Fifteen
The Yangtze Flows into the Sea

The Wanshou Pagoda in Jingzhou city

On the bank of the Yangtze River there is a pagoda, intended to tame the water, which was built over 400 years ago. While this is people's own wishful thinking, it is actually the embankment at the foot of the pagoda that deters any encroaching flood.

The oldest embankment along the Yangtze River was built in Jingzhou during the East Jin Dynasty. Guarding the most legendary city along the Yangtze River, it is mentioned in 72 of 120 chapters in The Romance of the Three Kingdoms. It has been lengthened and reinforced periodically ever since.

The Chu Culture had been thriving before heroic figures in the Three Kingdoms period arrived at the city. The ancient city of Jinan, just five kilometers north of Jingzhou, served as the capitol of the Chu Kingdom for 411 years, during the Spring and Autumn Period as well as the Warring States Period. Wealth and strategic location on the Yangtze River made Jingzhou a bone of contention in all wars. Because Jingzhou was so famous, the section of the Yangtze River between Zhicheng, Hubei Province and Chenglingji, Hunan Province was named the Jin River. Accordingly, the ancient embankment was referred to as the Jin River Embankment.

On the map there are 180 plus kilometers between Zhicheng and Chenglingji, but in reality the Jin River makes a notable eighteen turns, major or minor, within a stretch of 337 kilometers.

The setting sun above the Dongting Lake

Rivers wind freely through low-lying areas. Once the Yangtze River breaks away from the gorges in the upper reaches, it zigzags at will through the easily washed out sandy soil.

After the Nanjin Pass, there are no more narrow gorges along the middle and lower reaches; the Yangtze River rushes into a vast plain. The drop of a mere 50 meters within a distance of 1,854 kilometers between Yichang and the river mouth is in sharp contrast with the 5,400-meter fall in the upper reaches.

With the hard rocks near Chenglingji reining in the river to some extent, the water course straightens out. This is where the Jin River ends, and where the Yangtze River and Dongting Lake converge. Every year the Dongting Lake empties about eight billion cubic meters of water into the Yangtze River; the first major replenishment on its middle reaches.

The Dongting Lake used to be China's largest freshwater lake. About 250 million years ago, overflow from the Yangtze River and other rivers in the region was attracted to the existing low-lying basin to form the lake. Consequently the lake and the Yangtze River relieve each other of extra volume.

Lakes connected to rivers like this are known as tributary lakes. Four rivers supply the Dongting Lake. They are: the Xiang, Zi, Yuan, and Li Rivers. They flow into the Dongting River from all directions, resulting in the immense Dongting Lake water system that

The Yueyang Tower

The West Water Gate of the ancient Yueyang City

facilitates the flow of people and goods between the Yangtze and the entire Province of Hunan.

Some people describe the geographical relationship between the Dongting Lake water system and the Yangtze River as "connecting the Wu Gorge with Hunan Province". A large waterborne troop was created at such a strategic location. In 208 AD, the first ever large-scale fight on water took place at Chibi on the bank of the Yangtze River. After the battle Liu Bei, who had wandered from place to place, got hold of Jinzhou, consolidated his power, and entered into a tri-party confrontation against Cao Cao and Sun Quan.

Xiangfan, another ancient city over 100 kilometers away from Jinzhou, is of even greater strategic importance. Located on the banks of the Han River, it was used by Cao Cao to contain Liu Bei and Sun Quan. From a strategist's point of view, Xiangfan is right in the middle of China, where armies could set off to conquer the Central Plains to the north, Sichuan to the west and likewise, everything south of the Yangtze River thereby controlling the entire mainland.

During the Three Kingdoms' period, Lu Su, a general of the Wu Kingdom, had a watchtower built within 4,000 meters from where the Dongting Lake empties into the Yangtze River to inspect his waterborne troops. When peace returned, people found it to have the best view of the vast Dongting Lake. Consequently, it was repaired and renovated several times becoming what is now known as the Yueyang Tower. Fan Zhongyan, an eminent writer in the Northern Song Dynasty, wrote in *Note on The Yueyang Tower* that the Dongting Lake "merges seamlessly with distant mountains and the Yangtze River, vast and stretching to the horizon, assuming myriads of appearances as the lights change throughout the day".

Within a short distance to the north of the Yueyang Tower was the west gate of the ancient Yueyang City, a port of call for all ships. Busy water traffic made the west gate, not the south gate, the most important and bustling gate of the ancient city, a deviation from tradition that would never have occurred without the Dongting Lake "connecting the Wu Gorge with Hunan Province".

The Huanghe (Yellow Crane) Tower at Wuhan echoes the Yueyang Tower at a distance to its east. Together with the Tenwang Pavilion in Jiangxi Province and the Penglai Pavilion in Shandong Province, they are the four most famous towers in ancient China. The Han River joins the Yangtze River across from the Huanghe Tower.

Originating from the Qinling Mountains, the mainstream Han River flows 1,577 kilometers across Shaanxi Province and Hubei Province. It has the largest volume and widest drainage area of all tributaries in the middle and lower reaches of the Yangtze River. The confluence of the Han River and Yangtze River divides the city of Wuhan into three parts, hence the name Hankou (meaning the "estuary of the Han River").

Wuhan is "placed in the middle" in many senses in China. It is located in central China as well as the mid section in the middle reaches of the Yangtze River. Its unique geographic location allows Wuhan natives to access all parts of China via the Yangtze and Han Rivers.

Since ancient times this place has served as the major flood basin of the Yangtze. When poet Li Bai of the Tang Dynasty was here he exclaimed that "the mountains end where the plain begins and the great river joins a vast lake." For a long time Wuhan was surrounded by a huge wetland of which the ancient Yunmeng Lake, which no longer exists, was a part. Back then the wetland helped regulate the water level in the Yangtze River in flood seasons, sparing the surrounding areas from flood damage. The East Lake in Wuhan, China's largest lake within urban confines is a vestige of that wetland.

So far there are 164 bridges spanning the 6,383-kilometer Yangtze River, including the ones at Nanjing, Wuhu, Jiangyin and Yangzhou. They facilitate land-bound transportation across the great river.

At the confluence of the Yangtze River and the Han River, lies the 30,000-square-kilometer-plus Jianghan Plain. Together with the 10,000-square-kilometer-plus Dongting Plain to the south of the Yangtze River, it forms the so-called Hunan and Hubei Plain.

The Hunan and Hubei Plain borders the Boyang Lake Plain. Both are diluvian plains formed by silt from the Yangtze River and its tributaries. China's largest freshwater lake, the Boyang, lies in the center of the Boyang Lake Plain.

This is one of the largest habitats for migratory birds in the world. Every October tens of thousands of birds will invariably arrive at the Boyang Lake Migratory Bird Preserve and stay through the long winter at the vast lake. They come from Qinghai or Heilongjian thousands of miles away, or even further, from Siberia.

More than 150 species of migratory birds spend their winter here, including over 2,000 white cranes (95% of the total white crane population in the world). These hovering spirits are part of the spectacular scene at the Boyang Lake in the cold of winter.

As China's largest freshwater lake, the Boyang Lake stores three times more water than Dongting Lake, hence becoming the most important tributary lake of the Yangtze River. The Boyang Lake has maintained a relatively intact ecological system thanks to less human activities in the area. While the upper reaches of the Yangtze River enjoys a great many tributaries, the middle and lower reaches have access to the five major fresh lakes in China—the Dongting, Boyang, Chao, Tai, and Hongze Lakes.

The five freshwater lakes are to the Yangtze River what lungs are to the human body. They supply water to it and take in surplus from it in flood seasons, which they will hold until after the flood. The larger capacity a lake has, the better it is at regulating water levels.

The Boyang Lake

The Boyang Lake joins the Yangtze River at Hukou County, Jiujiang, Jiangxi Province. The name Jiujiang (meaning "nine rivers" in Chinese) is derived from the tributaries of the Boyang Lake. The Gan, Fu, Xin, Rao, and the Xiu Rivers, which feed the Boyang Lake, are known as the Five Rivers of the Boyang Lake.

The distribution map of the five major fresh lakes of the Yangtze River reaches

Among them, the Gan River, which flows across central Jiangxi from the south to the north, is the largest in the Boyang Lake water system. The five rivers are in turn fed by nine tributaries, hence the name of the city "Jiujiang".

The city of Jiujiang was created more than 2,000 years ago. Located at the exact spot where the four provinces of Jiangxi, Hubei, Hunan and Anhui meet, it is the only port city in Jiangxi.

The lower reaches of the Yangtze River begin at Hukou County, Jiujiang. The Shizhong Mountain at Hukou County, Jiujiang, has become famous after Su Dongpo wrote the famous *Note on Shizhong Mountain*. Here, the water volume of the Yangtze River increases drastically thanks to the contribution from the Boyang Lake. Despite its altitude of a mere 67.7 meters above sea level, the Zhizhong Mountain demarcates the middle and the lower reaches of the Yangtze River as it is here that the water level rises considerably.

Hukou is of great geological importance to the Yangtze River. It is the third major turning point for the great river. The run of geological fault zones forces the Yangtze River to make four major turns on its 6,380-kilometer journey towards the sea.

At Stone Drum Town, Lijiang in the upper reaches is the famous "First Bend of the Yangtze River". As the Dongting Lake joins the Yangtze in the middle reaches, the river changes its northwest-southeast course into a southwest northeast course, and then reverts to a northwest-southeast course near Wuhan, creating the "Second Bend of the Yangtze River". The river course changes a third time at Hukou, Jiujiang where the lower reaches start. After a final eastward bend near Nanjing, the course straightens out until it reaches the sea.

Between Wuhu and Nanjing, before the fourth turn, the river course inclines

The Jiujiang part of the Yangtze River

toward the northeast. As a result the literati used to call the south bank of the Yangtze River "River East" and the north bank, the "Left Bank". More than 2,000 years ago, Xiang Yu, a warlord of West Chu, killed himself with a sword instead of going into exile in "River East" across the Yangtze at Wujiang Town between Wuhu and Nanjing.

The Qingyi River, the first tributary of the Yangtze River in its lower reaches, joins the latter at Wuhu. It rises from Yi County, Huangshan, Anhui Province and has a length of 275 kilometers. This relatively short river connects eastern Jiangxi Province, southern Anhui Province and the vast region of ancient Huizhou. The famous Huizhou merchants reached Wuhu in the north via the Qingyi River, and then Yangzhou via the Yangtze River, working wonders in the history of trade and commerce in China.

Trade and commerce have always been well developed in Wuhu. By the end of the Qing Dynasty it had already come up on top out of the four major rice markets in China whose grain transaction accounted for more than half of the national total. Today it has an annual handling capacity of over 20 million tons, and is an important port city along the Yangtze River accessible to 10,000-ton-plus ocean-going vessels.

This is the vestige of China's earliest canal dating back to 485 B.C. For the

The Wuhu Ancient Tower at the meeting point of the Qingyi River and the Yangtze River

sake of territorial expansion King Fuchai of the Wu Kingdom had a canal built to connect the Han City, which he had just seized, with the Huai River. As the workers dug what was later called the Han Canal, people also built a city. Yangzhou would later become the most prosperous metropolis along the canal.

The Beijing-Hangzhou Grand Canal people see in Yangzhou has a total length of 1,764 kilometers. The canal system resulted from long-term efforts between the Sui and Qing Dynasties. In 604 A.D., Emperor Yang of the Sui Dynasty renovated and enlarged part of the ancient Han Canal. In six years' time four sections of artificial waterway with a total length of over 2,000 kilometers was constructed to connect Luoyang in the North and Hangzhou in the South.

More than 600 years later Kublai Khan lengthened the old canal until it finally reached Beijing. The still active Beijing-Hangzhou Grand Canal connects the five water systems of the Hai, Yellow, Huai, Yangtze, and Qiantang Rivers. The Grand Canal traverses the center of ancient Yangzhou before joining the Yangtze River at the ancient ferry crossing of Guazhou. Zhenjiang begins from across the Yangtze.

When road transportation was underdeveloped, the Yangtze River and the Grand Canal channelled the flow of people and goods.

The Runyang Bridge on the Yangtze River connecting Zhenjiang with Yangzhou was open to traffic in 2005. At nearly 36 kilometers in length, it is at present the longest bridge in China. It shortens the travel time between

The starting point of the Grand Canal in Yangzhou

either banks of the Yangtze to over 20 minutes. Today, the ancient Grand Canal has been reduced to an ordinary route for short-distance transport. People opt for the burgeoning road system if they need to travel further.

A flyover bridge annexed to the Runyang Bridge was built on the Shiyezhou Island between Yangzhou and Zhenjiang. Covering an area of 44 square kilometers and just a bit larger than the Island of Macau, this island is the fourth largest one in the Yangtze River. Its situation in the middle of the river made the bridge building far easier.

Islands are formed when rivers flow gently in wide courses. A line from *The Book of Songs*, "Guan Guan sings the osprey on the river island", mentions exactly such shoals. Sand carried from the upper reaches by the Yangtze River has been deposited in the middle and lower reaches, giving rise to numerous shoals. The wider the water course, the gentler the water flow, the larger the sandbank.

Each year the Yangtze River transports 500 million tons of sand to the estuary. The sand has done more than creating hundreds of shoals in the midst of the Yangtze River. Without it the vast expanse of land near the estuary would be non-existent.

The Congming Island is the largest shoal in the midst of the Yangtze River as well as the largest estuary alluvial island in the world. Its total area of over 1,000 square kilometers has earned it the third place among all Chinese islands. Today the great Yangtze River rushes to the sea near the homes of more than 600,000 island inhabitants.

There is an episode known as "Flooding the Jinshan Temple" in the Chinese folklore of *The Legend of White Snake*, wherein Lady White Snake exercised her magic power to flood the Jinshan Temple at Zhenjiang with water from the Yangtze River. Legends are hard to prove, but six to seven thousand years ago the Yangtze River did pour into the sea near where Zhenjiang is today. This area was indeed submerged by the river. Over the 6,000 years as sediment in the Yangtze River increased, the estuary has been gradually pushed outward. This finally resulted in forming the largest alluvial plain along the Yangtze River, the Yangtze River Delta.

The estuary of the Yangtze River

This is the youngest piece of land in the Yangtze River Basin. Parts of it were formed several thousand years ago, while others, only hundreds of years ago. 6,000 years' time has indeed brought great changes to the world.

The Yangtze River Delta refers to the vast area of about 50,000 square kilometers east of Zhenjiang, north of the Hangzhou Bay and south of the Tongyang Canal. Zhenjiang, which used to be close to the estuary, is now on the west edge of the Yangtze River Delta.

The Huangpu River joins the Yangtze River at the east edge of the Yangtze River Delta, the last tributary of the Yangtze River on its journey towards the sea. At the confluence is Shanghai, a small fishing village in the Spring and Autumn Period but a thriving metropolis at present. The part of the Yangtze River Delta around Shanghai is the world's sixth largest mega-city region. Economists regard this area, the youngest geologically speaking, as the most viable in China, creating wealth beyond measure.

This is the latest addition to the continent at the Yangtze River estuary, the last gift the great river presents to people before it joins the sea.

From a drop of water in the glaciers of the Qinghai-Tibet Plateau, the Roof of the World, to a torrential river of life, this great river of 6,380 kilometers finally finds its way home to the sea.

Chapter Sixteen
Three Thousand Peaks in Zhangjiajie

Three Thousand Peaks shrouded in mist and cloud in Zhangjiajie

The Li River zigzags through mountains in north-western Hunan Province before joining the Dongting Lake, which in turn feeds the Yangtze River. The area where the Li River rises and flows is known as Zhangjiajie.

Located in western Hunan, Zhangjiajie is part of the Wuling Mountains. It borders on the Yunnan-Guizhou Plateau in the southwest, the vast Dongting Plain to both the east and the west, and the Yangtze River to the north. Unique geographical location gives rise to a superior ecological system.

The "jie" in "Zhangjiajie" means boundary and confine in Chinese, but to Zhangjiajie natives it also refers to tall mountains. Zhangjiajie remained obscure when people swarmed famous mountains and great rivers in China. It was not until the early 1980s that its beauty finally became known.

A group of hill-dwellers, all surnamed Zhang, are the people most closely connected with Zhangjiajie. Legend has it that the Zhangjiajie Mountains were known as the Qingyan Mountains long ago.

It is said that Liu Bang, the First Emperor of the Han Dynasty, started a wanton slaughter of people who had rendered outstanding service to him once he had consolidated his power. Bitterly disappointed, Zhang Liang, Marquis of Liu, decided to go into hiding. After some roundabout travelling, he arrived at the Qingyan Mountains, where people were living a simple and pristine life sheltered by mountains and well supplied with water. He settled down here to practice Daoism. His offspring went on living here, hence the Qingyan Mountains were renamed "Zhangjiajie (the Zhang's Mountains)".

There is a sheer fall of altitude in Zhangjiajie since it is located at the transition zone from the second tier to the third tier in China from a

The Heavenly Gate Hill

geographical sense. Such a location makes it ideal for wind, clouds, rain and snow to gather.

The Heavenly Gate Hill eight kilometers from the city of Zhangjiajie soars into the sky with precipices on all four sides. In the distance the huge hole through the rocky wall resembles a gate to Heaven. It was claimed that the "Heavenly Gate Hill is inaccessible to man and deity alike".

How did such a spectacular formation and view come into being? According to researchers: weather; erosion; fractures in the mountains and earthquakes have all had their impact throughout time.

The hole through the hill is the largest of its kind in the world. It is shrouded in mist and clouds all year round.

Interestingly, many scenic spots in Zhangjiajie allude to a lucky number in China, nine, wishful thinking coinciding with nature. Anyway the Heavenly Gate Hill is a prelude to Zhangjiajie.

If one looks down at the "Thoroughfare to Heaven" on the Heavenly Gate Hill after climbing all 999 steps, one will find that the highway leading up to the hill top makes 99 turns, reminding one of the saying that "there are nine stories in Heaven". Despite its total length of a mere 10.77 kilometers, the highway ascends steeply from 200 meters above sea level to 1,300 meters, true to its name of "No. 1 Wonder in Highways".

The area here is famous for its numerous stone columns and stone peaks formed out of rare quartzite. According to geologists Zhangjiajie, located between the Yunnan-Guizhou uplift and the Dongting Lake subsidence, has been impacted by both the uplifting and subsiding forces. Moreover, advanced karst topography and cuts made by surface water have also had their hand in

Thoroughfare to Heaven

forming so many fantastic peaks of various heights.

The pristine geological feature here is unique to the Yangtze River Basin, and the best preserved at that. Outsiders find the beauty of Zhangjiajie to be beyond words. How did Nature create such a wonder in the first place?

Scientists say that there was an ocean here about 380 million years ago. The remains of a huge number of halo bios were reduced to dust, and then congealed to form quartzite about 520 meters in thickness. As the earth span around and its crust rose and fell, Zhangjiajie finally soared and came to a rest far above the sea surface.

Sedimentary rocks in Zhangjiajie have survived the force of change in their world, their grains the vestiges of quartz grits and creature remains that have been repeatedly washed by sea water.

Nature worked wonders with the bare broken quartzite throughout billions of years of time. Gravity turned mesas into canyons. Running water, floods, wind, frost, rain and snow sculptured hills and cliffs. Nature itself proves to be a great master in creating the uncanny beauty of Zhangjiajie.

Looking down from the Yaozi Village on the top of a hill, one sees a gentle stream winding its way through the green mountainous region like a stretch of white silk. This stream is inseparable from a peak, with which it even shares a name. The peak is called the Golden Whip Peak, and the stream, the Golden Whip Stream.

Tall ancient trees grow on both banks of the Golden Whip Stream. According to a poet, "The limpid water and verdant mountains are worthy of a painter's brush. One walks here like an immortal in a painting, each step revealing something even more refreshing."

By now Zhangjiajie is a renowned tourist attraction for both domestic and international travellers. Zhangjiajie has all classical geological features such as peaks, forests, caves, lakes and waterfalls. As one takes in the mountains one can hardly ignore the

Three Thousand Peaks in Zhangjiajie

The sedimentary rocks

streams. Altogether there are 3,000 peaks and 800 streams in Zhangjiajie. The 800 silvery streams string the 3,000 peaks together. If the peaks are compared to the body of Zhangjiajie, then the streams are its soul.

Among the green mountains and blue waters the Baofeng Lake is reputed to be the pearl on the crown. A reservoir with a maximum depth of 100 meters was formed solely by drops of spring water from the surrounding tall mountains. It is the magic water from high up that has created such a pearl so lovingly cradled by mountains.

Famed as "a scaled-up bonsai, a miniature wonderland and a gigantic garden", Zhangjiajie boasts over 300 scenic spots such as the Tianzi Mountain, the Huangshi Village, Yuanjiajie and the Golden Whip Stream. Can you imagine that there is still another wonderland beneath those towering peaks?

The Yellow Dragon Cave is a typical karst cave. Countless other caves similar to it still remain unexplored in Zhangjiajie. They date back as far as tens or even

The Golden Whip Lake

Zhangjiajie Waterfalls

hundreds of millions of years ago.

The most prominent sight inside the Yellow Dragon Cave is a 20.7-meter-long and 200,000-year-old stalactite. Right now there is a six-meter gap between its top and the roof of the cave. However, it will take another 60,000 years before the gap is closed.

The Baofeng Lake

One may count all 3,000 peaks outside the cave, but not the countless stalactites and stalagmites inside the cave.

Water plays an important role in the formation of these stalactites. Comparable to blood oozing out of rocks, it drips from overhanging stalactites to feed the stalagmites that are reaching up. Calcium carbonate in water is left behind to lengthen the stalactites so that eventually they meet. Water is the master hand driving this methodical and artistic process.

Although the ethnic Tu people have no written language of their own, the "primitive songs" sung by their ancestors when going out for battles have been passed on by word of mouth, which later evolved into Sangzhi Folk Songs. Wherever you go in Zhangjiajie, you can always hear ethic Tu girls sing.

Climate changes drastically on different terrains of Zhangjiajie. "One may experience four seasons in a day and the weather changes every ten li." Zhangjiajie is at its best in autumn, when Mother Nature paints the green mountains anew with bright colors.

It is not that cold in winter in Zhangjiajie. If there is snow, be it heavy or light, the scenery will look like an elegant Chinese wash painting. Snow gathered on withered branches or hilltops form a sharp contrast in color with the steep hills, reminding one of a line of ancient poetry, "Moss is the leaf of spring, and snow is the flower of winter."

Ancient waterwheels spin tirelessly to propel river water into the green fields. Ethnic Tu people live on river banks; their attachment to nature is reminiscent of the simplicity in ancient agrarian society.

Wangjiaping Village

Opinions differ as to the origin of the ethnic Tu people. Some say that in ancient times the Ba people living along the Qing River at the Three Gorges area fled the adverse environment there via the Yangtze River to the Wuling Mountains, where they integrated with the native dwellers to start the Tu ethnic group.

Houses supported by wooden stakes (or stilts) over ground, also known as "stiled houses" or "fence-style houses", dates back ages. Since there is far more hill land than farmland in Zhangjiajie, stiled houses become the natural choice for people wanting to make the most of slopes.

Houses supported by wooden stakes over grounds are the typical architectural style known to the ethnic Tu people. Mostly made from timber, the entire house is supported by several wooden stakes.

The stiled house usually leans on a hill and faces an open stretch of land.

The stalactice in the Yellow Dragon Cave

There are often narrow verandas facing the water source, which provide a nice view as well as a place to enjoy the cool. Seen from a distance, the houses merge seamlessly into the surroundings. After generations of efforts, there are now clusters of stiled houses, beautiful in special layout, depth and skyline.

Zhangjiajie is heaven to birds as well. Thanks to recent attention paid to

The sailors on the Li River

environmental protection, flocks of birds are happy to make their home in the dense woods here.

Birds are common motifs in the ethnic Tu culture. Xi Lan Ka Pu, a classical ethnic Tu fabric, reveals the charm of the ethnic Tu culture to the fullest.

The ethnic Tu people follow the traditional practice of brocade making, and the women excel in cross-stitch work and embroidery. The patterns are usually in symmetric pairs, ranging from simpler ones like flowers, birds, trees and insects to more complicated ones. All of the patterns reflect the Tu interpretation of the symmetry of nature and beauty.

Since water is plentiful in Zhangjiajie, influences of water can be detected in people's daily life. Water carries culture, and the culture of water in Tu villages is as profound as the Li River. Nature endowed us with Zhangjiajie so that we can fully appreciate its most pristine beauty. It is our invaluable wealth to have such a refuge from the sound and fury of the modern world.

Water enlivens mountains, and the reflections of the impressive mountains add glamour to the water's surface. The people of Zhangjiajie follow the running water to the long Li River, and then to the 800-*li* Dongting Lake to see the Yangtze River, whose song is already resounding inside them.

Ethnic Tu senior women of are weaving Xi Lan Ka Pu

Chapter Seventeen
Wuhan on Rivers and Lakes

Basking in the sun is a city, or more accurately, a combination of three prospering towns—Wuchang, Hankou and Hanyang. This is Wuhan, the mega city of the middle reaches of the Yangtze River.

Each busy morning in Wuhan starts with the breakfast stalls selling hot dried noodles, which are gobbled up by most of the locals along their way to a busy day.

Since the Yangtze River transverses the city, many local residents regard it as the center of Wuhan. Despite the well developed transportation system in Wuhan, the hundred-year-old ferries are still in use. The mode of travel hasn't changed nearly as much as the view from what it was a hundred years ago. The Wuhan Customs House, which used to be visible in the distance, is indistinguishable until the boats pull in.

One of the "Four Furnaces" in China, Wuhan is muggy from the onset of the rainy season in the late spring spanning through the early summer. The end of the rainy season signals the beginning of the Yangtze River flood season.

Wuhan residents don't feel much stress about the annual Yangtze River flood season. To them the water lines reported in the flood season are simply jargon used by hydrologists. If they want to know whether the river is flowing or ebbing, they simply count the number of stone steps still above water.

To senior citizens here there is no point discussing Wuhan without mentioning the river. To them the city and the river are inseparable.

The earliest urban layout of Wuhan dates back 3,000 years. Wuchang and Hanyang are on both banks of the eastbound Yangtze River. However, about 530 years ago, the Han River, which originates from the Qinling Mountains 3,000 kilometers away, changed its course to join the Yangtze River at a

The three towns of Wuhan

different place. Hanyang, the latest addition to the city, was thereby created.

The new Han River estuary is called Hankou, where ships fully loaded with people and goods drew alongside each other at the relatively smooth sections of the Han River. Consequently docks, streets and markets emerged, including Hanzheng Street.

Today Hanzheng Street is noisy as ever where dialects of all places are heard. In September 1979, the largest small-commodity bazaar of its time in China was reopened in this 1,600-meter-long ancient street.

Even now Hankou, the expanded version of the Hanzheng Street market, is still known as a "dock". Therefore Hanzheng Street may well be compared to the soul of Hankou. Traders' culture is so robust in this prime business location that there is a saying which goes to the effect that sellers and buyers alike will favor "whatever goods sell fast in Hankou". Hanzheng Street has become a

Wuhan citizens love to eating the hot dried noodles.

People relaxing in a cool place under the Wuchang Bridge

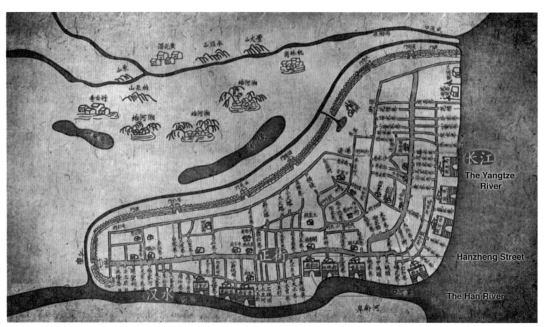

The schematic picture of the Hankou Town in the 1800s

symbol of the city's commerce.

Merchants gather here as their counterparts did several hundred years ago, but they won't be interested in the history of these ancient streets.

Where there is a dyke, there is a river. Hankou grew as each of the three successive dykes was built. In 1635, during the late Ming Dynasty, the first dyke was built along the Han River, giving rise to Zheng Street. In 1864 during the reign of Emperor Tongzhi of the Qing Dynasty, the local government built the Hankou Fort in the marsh beyond the first dyke, thus tripling the area of Hankou.

What turned Hankou into a modern city was the 17-kilometer long Zhanggong Dyke. In 1905, Zhang Zhidong, the then Governor General of Hunan and Hubei, led the efforts to build a dyke to better contain floods attacking Hankou. The dyke was renamed Zhanggong Dyke ("Honorable Mr. Zhang's Dyke" in Chinese) in his memory.

In the early 20th century smoke stacks from the largest steel complex of its time in Asia started puffing in

Hanyang Steel Factory

The Zhongshan Avenue in a huge flood in 1931

The Wuhan citizens were reinforcing the city dyke in 1954.

Wuhan, and steam whistles of the Beijing-Hankou trains wailed long and loud. Wuhan, a city in the middle reaches of the Yangtze River, caught the world's attention.

During this period, trading ports run by the Chinese stood side to side with docks in concession areas under foreign control along the Yangtze River in Hankou, and the traffic on the Beijing-Wuhan Railway was heavy. Wuhan evolved as its influence expanded from the Han River to the Yangtze River. It took Hankou only 500 years to overtake Wuchang and Hanyang, both possessing thousands of years' history, in fame and prosperity. The area was nicknamed the "Chicago of the East".

It was convenient water transportation via both the Yangtze River and the Han River that made it feasible for Wuhan to comprise the three parts. Supporting the city is the Jianghan Plain, known as a "Land of Abundance".

The rich and prosperous Jianghan Plain stimulated the miraculous boom in Wuhan for more than half a century. However, the great river seems to have a long memory. It may revert to a former course at certain time periods, one of which fell in the summer of 1931.

The 1931 Yangtze River flood, during which ships could sail on Hankou's Zhongshan Avenue, wiped out 500 years of Hankou's city-building efforts within a mere two months.

According to historical records there was a major flood in the Yangtze River every ten years. Other than building a higher and higher dyke, the only thing people could do was to pray. This Wanshou Pagoda in Jingzhou, built

The Wuhan Yangtze River bridge

over 450 years earlier during the Ming Dynasty, was meant to tame floods. Its foundation is now 7.9 meters away from the Jingjiang Dyke.

The water-taming iron ox placed in 1788 during the reign of Emperor Qianlong of the Qing Dynasty was washed away by a flood. The iron ox seen today was cast in 1859 during the reign of Emperor Xianfeng of the Qing Dynasty.

Although those water-taming devices turned out to be ineffective, they help illustrate the recognized importance of something that was the Jingjiang Dyke. The entire Jianghan Plain will be flooded if it bursts. That was why an earthen dyke was built in as early as the East Jin Dynasty over 1,600 years ago, which was fortified and extended, evolving into the 182-kilometer Jingjiang Dyke of today.

On October 15th 1957, the opening ceremony of the Wuhan-Yangtze River Bridge

In 1957 the first ever bridge spanning the Yangtze River was built in Wuhan. Together with the Han River No. 1 Bridge completed in 1956, it linked the three parts of Wuhan and put an end to the inconvenience caused by train ferries on the Beijing-Guangzhou Railway.

Thanks to the Jingjiang flood-diversion project as well as the bridges, the Yangtze River and the Beijing-Guangzhou Railway are now connected. Wuhan has earned its reputation as a city with easy access to nine provinces. The Greater Wuhan region shaped by the Yangtze and Han Rivers is rising again as a mega city for the middle reaches of the Yangtze and beyond to all of central China.

Wuhan Customs House

Wuhan residents enjoy swimming in the Yangtze River and the Han River. For them to swim is to "play with water".

Finished in 1924, the Wuhan Customs House used to be the symbol of Wuhan. It was still the tallest building in town twenty years ago, but now it is just one of the many buildings in the city's skyline.

Similarly, the single bridge spanning the Yangtze River twenty years ago is now facing competition from six other bridges either completed or under construction. Time and history seem to be embodied in these bridges, each with its own stories to tell.

If the bridges are said to be symbols of water standing still; the water running beneath them is also a fluid bridge bringing people and goods from all directions together. Both of them add a dynamic optimism to the city of Wuhan.

White clouds hover above the 30-square-kilometer East Lake. Wuhan ranks No. 1 in per capita freshwater resource among all big cities in the world. Wuhan residents take the joy in being able to play with water in China's greatest river and row boats in China's largest urban lake.

The river water is tinted golden by first rays of the morning sun. A new day begins at Wuhan, a city on rivers and lakes.

Chapter Eighteen
Taoist Wudang Mountain

As a native Chinese religion, Daoism spread widely along the Yangtze River. Consequently there are four major Daoist Mountains in the Yangtze River Basin: Qingcheng Mountain, Wudang Mountain, Dragon and Tiger Mountain, and Qiyun Mountain. Although recluses started practicing Daoism on Wudang Mountain quite early in time, its influence peaked in the Ming Dynasty.

In 1417, Zhu Di, or Emperor Yongle of the Ming Dynasty, arrived in Beijing as the construction of the Forbidden City in Beijing entered its second year.

Upon seeing the spectacular construction site, he had another vision. Soon an imperial edict was issued to Wudang Mountain over 1,000 kilometers away, in which the Emperor conferred the title of "Taihe Palace of Supreme Harmony on the Master Mountain" on a Daoist palace on the mountain.

In the 19 years between 1405 and 1424, Emperor Yongle issued altogether more than 60 edicts to Wudang Mountain in the south.

As the Yangtze River approaches the Hunan and Hubei Plain in its middle reaches, its largest tributary, the Han River, joins hands with it. Wudang Mountain, which covers an area of 400 square kilometers, stands lofty and proud at Shiyan, Hubei Province to the west of the Han River.

By the time Emperor Yongle actually set foot on the Forbidden City in Beijing, construction here had been going on for five years.

The "Taihe Palace of Supreme Harmony on the Master Mountain"

The architectural complex on the Wudang Mountain

At that time construction on Wudang Mountain was in full swing. Why did the relatively out-of-the-way mountain attract such great attention from the Emperor? Originally named Taihe Mountain, Wudang Mountain had Daoist temples to worship the god Xuan Wu who ascended to Heaven right here in ancient times. It was later renamed Wudang Mountain by taking two characters out of the saying that "only Xuan Wu is worthy ('Dang' in Chinese) of the mountain."

It was exactly because of god Xuan Wu, also known as god Zhen Wu, that Emperor Yongle issued two edicts in a single month in spring 1412, ordering architecture with "size and shape proper to the mountain". A grand project was thus launched.

Emperor Yongle wasn't seized by a whim. In fact in the prior year he had assigned officials to the mountain to raise money, and ordered the purchase of 100,000 units of timber from such places as Sichuan.

On September 18th of the Chinese lunar calendar in 1412, the construction of Daoist palaces and temples were officially kicked off as soldiers and craftsmen from the Forbidden City in Beijing as well as close to 300,000 corvee workers from south of the Yangtze River arrived at Wudang Mountain. This was the largest national project in the entire Ming Dynasty in terms of both duration and scale. Historical annals put it in this way, "There is the construction of the Imperial Palace in the north and the construction on

The Purple Cloud Palace

Wudang Mountain in the south."

The project turned out to be massive and arduous. Craftsmen from the Forbidden City in Beijing were transported speedily from the North China Plain to the verges of gorges and cliffs of Wudang Mountain. Although the blueprint in their hands was simply a duplication of palaces in Beijing, it was far more difficult to realize in such an environment. Moreover, it never occurred to them that they were to spend more than ten years or even their entire life here.

Today Wudang Mountain is a famous tourist attraction listed as one of the World Cultural Heritage sites.

The Purple Cloud Palace on Wudang Mountain is reputed to be a dwelling of immortals.

The Dragon and Tiger Hall lies right beyond the Golden River. On the other side of the Dragon and Tiger Hall are steps leading up to the Worship Hall dozens of meters higher. Along the steps are pairs of pavilions for sheltering stone tablets. Going out of the back of the Worship Hall one finds the bright open Purple Cloud Square, where the Purple Cloud Hall towers aloft on a tall three-storied platform.

The best preserved wooden structure on Wudang Mountain, the Purple Cloud Hall is also an important venue for the worship of god Zhen Wu. As the sun rises, the Daoist morning mass begins.

The Daoist music played here is a fusion of the southern school and the northern school. As solemn and elegant as court music, it is said to have been

The plan of the Crown Prince Slope

played for hundreds of years.

With the start of the music of the morning mass, the door of the Purple Cloud Palace opens to welcome waves of Daoist believers and tourists. The visitors hail from many countries and regions and choose the Purple Cloud Palace as the first stop in their Wudang Mountain experience.

On the hall ceiling, Eight Diagrams were painted on both sides of a central coffer with images which two dragons playing with a pearl. All these markings bespeak imperial power.

An aerial view of the Purple Cloud Palace reveals a perfectly straight central axis, which tallies with the Ming Dynasty principle of "imperial power is located along the central axis".

Obviously construction workers from Beijing saw imperial will in the blueprint they had been given, so they built grand walls, steps, courtyards, and halls in a precisely symmetric pattern.

Most of the magnificent buildings on Wudang Mountain were built gradually up slopes in a symmetric pattern on either side of the central axis. The Purple Cloud Palace faces the south while leaning on the Flag Unfolding Peak. This positioning embodies the ancient Chinese feng shui principle of "embracing the sun and having the back towards shady spots, facing the water and leaning against the mountain". Following the principles are said to be conducive to the formation and preservation of a field of *qi*, or vital energy, an essential element of feng shui.

The best known Wudang Kongfu is Taijiquan, or Chinese shadow boxing. The movements and postures in it balance fastness with slowness and gentleness with firmness. Said to be the best kind of Kongfu to keep fit, it has close to 500 million followers around the world.

Abundant energy in the environment here helps preserve health, a highlight of Wudang Kongfu. Take a deep breath, calm down; your mind, eyes and hands are all one. This is the integration with nature they seek.

Follow the floating clouds and running streams, your hands move continuously in the wilderness. This is integration with nature too.

Architecture at the Fuzhen Daoist Temple, also known as the Crown Prince Slope, seems to have violated the Wudang Mountain principle of "imperial power is located along the central axis".

A comparison with other palaces and temples show that a central axis is not feasible on the narrow Crown Prince Slope, which explains why buildings scatter left and right on this particular site.

Such design changes are not made up by us. In fact, when engineers and technicians arrived from Beijing, they brought with them not only a blueprint, but also an imperial edict from Emperor Yongle, "You shall not make any alteration to the mountain itself."

Buildings on the Crown Prince Slope start halfway up the mountain. Right beyond the gate of the temple there is a winding covered corridor built along the slope. One can well imagine that back then, as architects and engineers revised the layout, they also changed the entrance and passageway of this compound. To one's amazement, this winding covered corridor carries sound waves like the Echo Wall in the Temple of Heaven in Beijing. People gave it a special name, the Zigzag Passage.

Beyond the temple gate and a second gate stands the Dragon and Tiger Hall, through whose door the main building of the Crown Prince Slope is visible. However, one has to go through several gates before reaching the next compound, hence the saying that "there are four gates in a single *li*."

Although there are five stories in the Five Clouds Hall, one steps onto the highest floor upon entry. What a nice feeling to have reached the top in one step! At one side of the hall 12 crossbeams are stacked on an upright wooden pillar, which is the famous "12 Crossbeams on a Pillar" of the Crown Prince Slope. Why such a structure? Was it the result of the difficulty of construction or something else?

The structural of the "12 Crossbeams on a Pillar" of the Crown Prince Slope

It turns out that the Five Clouds Hall is located on a slope. Digging into the mountain or levelling up the slope would violate the edict of "You shall not make any alteration to the mountain itself." Consequently engineers came up with "12 Crossbeams on a Pillar."

Architecture here suits the terrain. There are buildings on slopes as well as hill tops, a distinctive feature of Wudang Mountain architecture.

The Purple Cloud Palace leans against the Flag Unfolding Peak. Out of its exit one see a simple mottled stone doorway standing serenely half way up the Flag Unfolding Peak.

A mountain path at the back of the Crown Prince Rock leads to the Crown Prince Cave. Amazingly, a stream of spring water oozes out of the rock face and drops right into an ancient well in front of the cave, as if the thin thread of droplets connected heaven and earth. The young Zhen Wu was said to have devoted himself to decades of strict religious discipline in order to achieve immortality.

The precipitous Southern Rock is reputed to be the most beautiful of all 36 rocks on Wudang Mountain.

It is precipitous because there is a fault in the mountain. It is astounding to see the Southern Rock Palace hanging on the sheer cliff like a painting on the wall.

The geological conditions here are quite unique. The byway carved out of the cliff, which has a sheer drop of several hundred meters, was an obvious temptation to adventurers. What came to the mind of architects and engineers working for Emperor Yongle when they got here? How did they manage to embed building materials into the hard rock face? Their achievements have left

The Southern Rock

later generations in awe and wonder.

Fifteen types of workers were sent from Beijing, one of which was "scaffolding workers". Without the scaffolds they set up, the Southern Rock Palace would not have been built.

On the Southern Rock there is a dragon head carved out of the cliff face which looks down into a bottomless pit. Devout religious believers used to venture there to burn incense although they were fully aware that they might fall into the pit and never come back, because they thought incense burnt here would reach the gods in Heaven.

Designers and engineers back then couldn't have built the so-called "Dragon

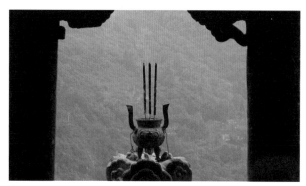

The "Dragon Head Altar" of the Southern Rock Palace

Head Altar" to lure people to lose their lives, so why was this precise spot chosen? If one looks up from the Dragon Head Altar, one would realize that the location was chosen because it was directly opposite the highest peak of Wudang Mountain, the Golden Summit, or the Heavenly Pillar Peak.

One has to climb ten kilometers to

The animal sculptures on the ridge of the roof of the Gilded Hall

reach the Golden Summit from the Southern Rock. It's not hard to imagine the difficulty in construction.

Standing on the misty peak and gazing into the surrounding hills, what kind of mysterious spiritual experience did those craftsmen, kept away from their hometown, go through?

In order to reach the peak, craftsmen paved the so-called "Holy Passage" with flagstones in addition to planked roads built along valleys. Stone steps lead up to the peak, and buildings of all sizes are arranged to suit the terrain. They bring out the rugged mountain even more.

The Heavenly Pillar Peak, the highest peak of Wudang Mountain, soars 1,612 meters above sea level.

All Ming Dynasty building efforts radiated from the Heavenly Pillar Peak. The middle section and top of the steep peak were designated as the places where god Zhen Wu was canonized, and where he ruled, respectively. The world of immortals was recreated here.

The height desired by Emperor Yongle posed the greatest challenge to construction workers. This had to be done systematically. In the materials yard at the foot of hills or on plank roads along cliffs, craftsmen and corvee workers erected beams and houses, smelted copper or iron. Architecture situated in such an environment demonstrated the power of religion as well as a more profound influence.

Supported by a 160-square-meter platform, the Gilded Copper Hall on top of the Heavenly Pillar Peak got its name because it was cast entirely out of copper and gold.

How on earth was this largest gilded copper architecture in China cast? Was it cast in one piece or separately? The answers were not found until the late 1980s.

On the ninth day of the ninth month on the Chinese lunar calendar in 1416, prefabricated components of the gilded hall made it to Wudang Mountain after travelling on the Beijing-Hangzhou Great Canal, the Yangtze River and the Han River. On site craftsmen assembled the pieces by inserting tenons into mortises in the same way they built wooden houses. Afterwards they smeared the structure with slurry of melted gold and mercury. Charcoal fires were then built to bake the slurry so that mercury evaporated, leaving a huge gilded copper hall on the hill top of the Heavenly Pillar Peak.

Today, if we look carefully at this pure metal structure, we can still indentify traces of assembly.

Since the gilded hall conducts electricity, it would be lit up and sparkling if stricken by thunder. This marvellous spectacle is known as "Thunder and Fire Tempering the Hall". Although built more than 500 years ago, the gilded hall is intact and dazzling as ever.

In order to protect the gilded hall, Emperor Zhongle issued an edict to build a wall similar to the one in the Forbidden City in Beijing around the Golden Summit. The "Purple City" came into being.

In 1417, Emperor Yongle issued another imperial edict, "The Gilded Hall on the summit shall be named Taihe Palace of Supreme Harmony on the Master Mountain."

The restored scene of "Thunder and Fire Tempering the Hall" of the Wudang Gilded Hall

The restored picture of the ancient Junzhou Town submerged under the Danjiangkou Reservoir

By then Wudang Mountain had recreated scenes in which Zhen Wu ascended to heaven, received canonization and assumed command of the world.

The size and shape of the gilded hall are identical with those of the Taihe Palace in the Forbidden City in Beijing. The statue of God Zhen Wu inside the hall was said to be modelled after Zhu Di. Consequently there is a folk saying of "God Zhen Wu in the image of Emperor Yongle."

Twelve years later, in 1424, all 33 building clusters belonging to the nine palaces and eight Daoist temples on Wudang Mountain were completed. Centered upon the Gilded Copper Hall, the nine palaces and eight temples, which were arranged along a 70-kilometer central axis, had a total floor space of 1.6 million square meters dedicated to performing Daoist rites for the royal family.

Wudang Mountain became "No. 1 Fairyland Under Heaven" in the Ming Dynasty. Emperor Yongle, the personification of God Zhen Wu, ensured the reign of the Ming Dynasty over both heaven and earth for more than 200 years.

The Danjiangkou Reservoir at the foot of Wudang Mountain is said to be the largest artificial lake in China. During its construction, which started from 1958, a thousand-year-old town, Junzhou, was submerged. The town, which used to be the starting point of Daoist buildings on Wudang Mountain constructed in the Ming Dynasty, was the first dot in a line connecting Wudang Mountain with the Forbidden City in Beijing.

Almost 600 years later, the clear river water, which carried thousands of ships in the past, will again flow towards Beijing with the launching of the Chinese projects of diverting water from the south to the north.

A new chapter in history has been turned.

Chapter Nineteen
Lushan, Mountain with Immortals' Houses

A mountain rises where the middle and lower reaches of the Yangtze River meet; atop the Lushan mountain shrouded in clouds is the small town of Guling.

Despite its nestled position, this is a town with all modern facilities. Neither local residents nor visitors can tell much difference between life down below and life high up.

The Chinese character "Lu" stands for "house", so Lushan literally means "a mountain with houses". When enough houses were built on the mountain, the town of Guling came into being, making it the only town located on a famous mountain in China.

More than 3,000 years ago, Kuang Su and his six brothers built huts on Lushan to practice Taoism. Eventually he attained immortality, leaving the huts behind for the spirit world. The mountain became known as the "mountain with immortals' houses", or simply put, Lushan.

The Guling Town

At an altitude of over 1,200 meters above sea level, this town is said to be the highest town along the Yangtze River. A saying goes that, "a mountain flew over and settled itself on the bank of the Yangtze River." From Lushan people can look down into the Yangtze River, the nearby Boyang freshwater Lake, and the strategic Jiujiang city.

Lushan borders on the Yangtze

The young Sterling

Sterling and his classmates on Lushan in 1934

The Sterling Family on Lushan in 1942

The Sterling couple in America in 2005

River to the north and the Boyang Lake to the east. The glistening lake sets off the imposing but enchanting backdrop of Lushan.

"Ridges or peaks; Lushan looks different from different perspectives. How could one tell what Lushan really looks like when one is in the mountain range?" Many people come to know Lushan because of this poem by Su Dongpo, the most beloved poem about Lushan.

More than 1,500 prominent figures in Chinese history from Sima Qian down to Tao Yuanming, Li Bai, Bai Juyi, Su Dongpo and Zhu Xi climbed Lushan to compose poems or build houses, their words leaving a rich cultural heritage for centuries that follow. During the 200 years between the reign of Emperor Kangxi and that of Emperor Guangxu of the Qing Dynasty, a growing number of foreigners also visited Lushan. Travellers, settlers, sages and poets; Lushan has won the heart of all people by its distinctive charm.

Like all other famous mountains in China, Lushan displays stone inscriptions from past ages all over its cliffs. However, this stone inscription in English engraved 100 years ago is unique to Lushan. It has become an indelible symbol of the cultural integration on Lushan.

Astounding discoveries are usually made by accident. As workers tore down a fireplace to renovate an old house for its new owner, a photo album yellowed by age fell down to the floor. The photos recorded the happy moments of this expatriate family 100 years before conveyed the effects of the life on Lushan deeply.

Both Sterling Whitener and his wife were born and raised on Lushan. Later the two childhood playmates got married and raised babies of their own on Lushan. The photos captured all their happy moments here.

In the first half of the 19th century, Western powers forced their way into China with their gunboat policy, turning Shanghai, Nanjing, Wuhan, Jiujiang and other cities along the Yangtze River into trading ports. Foreigners swarmed into those cities to live and work.

At that time expatriates living along the Yangtze River could hardly stand the summer heat in those cities. They wanted badly a summer resort that was cooler, beautiful and accessible. Lushan seemed to be an ideal choice.

The Five Elders Peak of Lushan is visible from Jiujiang. Not far away from the peak is the Jinxiu Valley. The mountain path at the bottom of the valley leads to the Pavilion Sheltering the Tablet with Imperial Inscriptions.

Zhu Yuanzhang, the First Emperor of the Ming Dynasty, insisted on building a pavilion on the uninhabited top of Lushan to house a stone tablet of his own inscriptions to pay homage to Crazy Monk Zhou. In order to transport the stone tablet uphill, workers built a rugged mountain road full of twists and turns.

In winter 1886, Edward Selby Little, a British missionary, travelled from Hankou down to Jiujiang via the Yangtze River. Upon landing he followed this mountain path to climb Lushan.

He was greatly shocked by Guling, a flat land on top of the mountain.

How would his marvel impact Lushan?

Edward Selby Little realized that he could set a trend among expatriates living in cities alongside the Yangtze River to spend summers on Lushan if he developed property in Guling,

The Pavilion sheltering the Tablet with Imperial Inscriptions

The Guest Greeting Pine on the Five Elders Peak

a place already known to Westerners for its cultural heritage, a place of mild temperature thanks to the high altitude, and a place readily accessible through water transportation on the Yangtze River.

Shrewd as he was, Edward Selby Little lost no time in leveraging the influence of Western powers to force through the lease of Guling for an incredibly long period of 999 years!

Edward Selby Little named the place "Cooling", which shares a similar pronunciation with the Chinese name "Guling".

Shortly afterwards Edward Selby Little started development on this piece of leased land by dividing it into lots and then sold to different countries. More than thirty churches from over twenty countries scrambled to buy lots from him to build houses on. Property development boomed on Lushan.

In twenty to thirty years' time over 560 villas of various styles had sprung up on Lushan. Today people can still have a general view of world architectural styles by visiting the area nicknamed "World Architecture Expo".

Here the Chinese culture interacts with the Western culture. Those exotic buildings are surrounded by the elegant scenery of Lushan and imbued with a deep flavor of traditional Chinese culture. For the next 100 years, Lushan continued to win the hearts of Westerners with its spectacular beauty and rich cultural heritage.

In Memories of Lushan American writer Pearl Buck recalled with affection

The Guling Town in the 1930s

her childhood on Lushan.

On April 6th 1991 an expert who had been living on Lushan for a long time discovered a tombstone on a deserted flagstone path between two villas. The tombstone inscription in English reads:

"Forever remembered in Love. Absalom Sydenstricker, born on August 13th 1852 in Rickwood, Virginia, and deceased on August 31st 1931 in Guling, Lushan, China."

Undoubtedly this is the tombstone of Pearl Buck's father Absalom Sydenstricker, one of the first Americans to build a house in Guling. In 1897 his simple little villa, at 310 Zhongsi Road, was completed.

It was in this villa that his daughter wrote the novel *The Good Earth*, for which she was awarded the 1938 Nobel Prize for Literature. The book was reputed to have "moved God" by its descriptions of the everyday life of Chinese peasants.

She gave herself a Chinese name as beautiful as the minds of the Chinese in her novels, Sai Zhenzhu ("Zhenzhu" meaning "pearl" in Chinese). She came to China when she was only three months' old, and aside from a break to attend college in the U.S., she spent nearly 40 years of the prime of her life in China. She spent the longest and most memorable time in her life on Lushan.

Accompanying her growth were church bells as well as gurgling springs. In the early 20th century, with the influx of expatriates, Catholic cathedrals, Christian and Orthodox churches and mosques were built alongside Buddhist temples and Daoist monasteries on Lushan. Lushan became a famous religious mountain accommodating six religions.

The Donglin Temple was built by Huiyuan, an eminent monk during the East Jin Dynasty 1,600 years ago. It was the birthplace of an important sect of Buddhism, the Jingtu Sect, or the Pure Land Sect.

There is a Buddhist temple at the foot of the Buddha's Hand Rock. Lü Dongbin is said to have attained immortality in a cave here. During the reign of Emperor

Villas on Lushan

Jiaqing of the Qing Dynasty, the temple was converted into a Taoist memorial of Lü Dongbin. Ever since then the cave has been known as the Fairy Cave.

After a tour of the cave in 1959, Mao Zedong wrote in a poem that "Nature has excelled herself in the Fairy Cave, on perilous peaks dwells beauty in her infinite variety." The Fairy Cave was immediately known throughout the country.

It is a wonder in the history of world cultures that six religions could keep peace with each other on a single mountain.

There are three important buildings constructed by Chinese hands on Lushan.

The first one is the Lushan Auditorium finished in 1937, where Mao Zedong chaired three successive meetings of political significance in 1937, 1959, and 1970, a special time period to Lushan.

The second one is the Lushan Library completed in July 1935. Although it does integrate some elements of Western architecture, it has the most outstanding characteristics of Chinese architecture among all buildings on Lushan. It was here that the Anti-Japanese War Declaration was issued, stating that "every person, living in the north or the south, young or old, should assume responsibilities for defending the homeland against Japanese aggression." The Lushan Library and the Anti-Japanese War Declaration have

Pearl Buck

Sydenstricker Couple

become a key part of maintaining the longevity of Chinese history.

The third building is the Meilu Villa formerly owned by Chiang Kai-shek and his wife Soong Mei-ling, where three paintings by the latter depicting three places the couple attached to sentimentally throughout their life—Fenghua, Nanjing and Lushan—are on display.

Lushan is of great value to scientific research, especially the distinctive vestiges of Quaternary glacier. Lushan was among the first batch of "World Geological Parks" acknowledged by UNESCO.

Lushan is also reputed to be a mountain with an atmosphere suited to deep learning. The spectacular views of Lushan and the rich traditional Chinese culture alike have left deep impressions on aspiring Chinese academics through the ages and even western kids growing up on Lushan from the early 20th century.

The White Deer Grotto Academy, established in the Tang Dynasty more than 1,000 years ago, is the oldest school on Lushan. Zhu Xi in the Song Dynasty over 800 years ago renovated it and developed it into the best of the top four academies of its time in China. The White Deer Grotto Academy

The French Catholic Church on Lushan

The British Christian Church on Lushan

The American Christian Church on Lushan

The Meilu Villa

Regulation penned by him was one of the earliest educational regulations in the world, a fact known to educators everywhere.

The Guling American School on Lushan was established in 1916. Its curriculum was a flexible combination of Western and Chinese learning. The teachers were responsible for teaching kids Chinese, along with a broad spectrum of traditional western subjects. The school taught traditional Chinese culture too. Kids could learn to perform traditional Chinese operas, and girls could take elective courses in Chinese cooking.

As the Japanese army approached Lushan, the Guling American School agreed to safeguard over 170 cases of botanical and rock specimens for the Lushan Botanical Garden, an act of righteousness forever recorded in history.

"The historical relics on Lushan are integrated in a distinctive way with outstanding natural beauty, creating sights of cultural interests that are of great aesthetic value and relevance to the Chinese national spirit and cultural life"— a comment made by the world on Lushan.

In 1996, Lushan became a part of the World Cultural Landscape.

The former site of the Guling American school

The group photo of students of Guling American School in 1932

Chapter Twenty
Huizhou, A Dreamland

The Baoguan Pavilion

Although ancestral halls are common in villages in south Anhui Province, one at Chengkan Village stands out because it has a pavilion modelled after the Confucian Temple in Shandong and the Taihe Palace in Beijing. This is the Baoguan Pavilion of the Dongshu Ancestral Hall at Chengkan Village; the history of one family is forever preserved inside those massive doors.

During the reign of Emperor Wanli of the Ming Dynasty, Luo Yinghe, the Supervisor of Official Conduct at that time, had this two-storied pavilion built at his hometown to store up imperial edicts and gifts, and to show off the honor and glory of his family. Situated on an out-of-the-way mountain, this pavilion was of a scope and construct far exceeding its owner's due.

Chengkan Village is cradled in a col more than 100 kilometers south of the Yangtze River. During the late Tang Dynasty, Luo's ancestors migrated from Jiangxi to this place surrounded by mountains and water to get away from the rampant waves of warfare in other regions. They named it Chengkan, which means "man and nature in one" in Chinese, in the hope of bringing luck to the family. The family has enjoyed that peace and luck they longed for; carrying on the family line, never to depart again.

According to historical records Chengkan Village boomed throughout

Chengkan Village

the Song, Yuan and Ming Dynasties. There were more than 110 government officials in the Luo family during the Ming Dynasty. The ancestors of Zhu Xi, a renowned idealist philosopher in the Song Dynasty, also lived in Chengkan.

This is an ancient village. Displaying its history are the over 130 buildings which date back to the Song, Yuan, Ming and Qing Dynasties. There are close to 100 crisscrossing lanes and two zigzagging ditches.

The former Huizhou area includes Huangshan, She County, Xiuning, Qimen, Jixi, and Yi County in present-day Anhui Province as well as Wuyuan in Jiangxi Province.

There is a saying about Huizhou that "mountains take up 70% of the area; water, 10%; and farmland, another 10%." Since the hilly land could hardly feed the huge population, many Huizhou natives had to make a living elsewhere. They found it more convenient to travel by water.

The 143-meter stone dam across the Lian River known as Yuliang Dam was initially constructed in the Sui Dynasty. During the Ming and Qing Dynasties, this area was a distributing

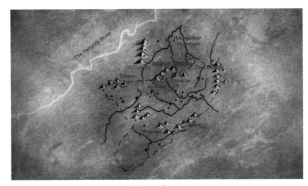

The ancient Huizhou area and the Yangtze River

The Yuliang Dam

center for cargoes going from Huizhou to Jiangsu and Zhejiang. Yuliang consequently became a cargo-handling dock.

Huizhou natives preferred to travel via the Taiping Lake into the Qingyi River, and then merged into the Yangtze River at Wuhu. For them it was a golden waterway leading as far west as Wuhan and as far east as Yangzhou.

Huizhou merchants had deep enough pockets to build a great number of memorial arches and ancestral halls to show off their glory. The famous "Three Consummate Skills" of wood carving, stone and brick engravings are applied in almost every house in Huizhou.

It is said that when Wang Dinggui, a major salt dealer of the Ming and Qing Dynasties, built the Chengzhi Hall at Hongcun Village, Yi County. He signed a long-term contract with master craftsmen who were skilful enough to carve seven to eight layers into a thin piece of timber or stone. The engraved dimensional figures and sceneries were so meticulously recreated that they seemed ready to come out at one's call.

Neither the devoted craftsmen nor their Huizhou merchant patrons could

Stone engraving

Brick engraving

Wood carving

The Chengzhi Hall at Hongcun village, Yi County

have expected that these three types of engravings would one day become recognized examples of World Cultural Heritage.

In 1985, an American studying in China travelled to Huizhou. Deeply impressed by the first encounter, she went to visit one village after another in Huizhou. Her name is Nancy Berliner.

After her sojourn in China Nancy became Curator of Chinese Art and Culture at the Peabody Essex Museum. As soon as she assumed her post she proposed relocating an ancient Huizhou house to the U.S for exhibition.

In 1996, Wang Shukai, a Chinese with many years' working experience in the U.S, arrived in Huizhou in the capacity of assistant to Nancy.

He started a complex and arduous selection process. Since rules and regulations concerned ban the sale of any protected houses, he could only choose from the more ordinary ones. After having spent over a year's time visiting all villages in Huizhou, he picked 600 houses out of over 1,000, then 60 out of the 600, and finally six out of the 60. Wang Shukai had a hard time deciding on a single house that could best represent Huizhou houses.

Huizhou houses

Since colored ornaments and tiers of brackets inserted between the top of a pillar and a crossbeam were banned

Caiyu Village of She County

in civilian houses in the Ming and Qing Dynasties, old houses in Huizhou kept a uniform appearance of grey bricks and white walls. Hiding everywhere inside the houses, however, were meticulous engravings.

Huizhou people were particular about furnishings too. They hang horizontal boards on walls inscribed with words of proclamation or blessing and place ornaments on long narrow tables to wish for peace and safety for family members who had to be away from home most time of the year.

Adherents of the idealist school of Confucianism, Huizhou merchants looked up to traditional culture. The peace of mind and elegance they sought can be detected in their houses.

Most old Huizhou houses are enclosed by high walls. The few windows in the wall are usually small. To Wang Shukai, such houses impress people as being gloomy and desolate.

Lighting and ventilation inside the house rely on uncovered skylights in courtyards. Moreover, the skylights are also part of the drainage system since rain water from the roofs is channelled into it. As a result locals also call those skylights "gathering places of all water". To them water symbolizes wealth and an ever-flourishing population.

One old house in Huizhou, the Yinyu Hall at Huangcun Village, Xiuning

County was finally chosen from amongst a thousand. Wang Shukai finally decided to take the dwelling of the 28th Huang patriarch, a hardworking pawnbroker merchant during the reign of Emperor Kangxi of the Qing Dynasty. Later, having made his fortune, he returned to his hometown to build a huge cluster of four compounds, each of which had five rooms in a row. In total, there were 16 bedrooms. He named it "Yinyu" because the word stood for "benefiting the offspring" in Chinese. Eight later generations of Huang's lived there. A lively compound for over 200 years, it was eventually deserted in the early 1980s. In 1997, or the second year Wang Shukai spent in Huizhou, the Yinyu Hall finally saw a return to its good fortune.

Photos of the Yinyu Hall had been taken before it was taken apart. In midsummer 1997, the 35th generation of Huangs bid farewell to their ancestral residence.

Disassembling such an old house turned out to be no easier than erecting a new one. Each and every roof tile or painting stuck to a wall had to be taken down with care.

In more than two months' time the old house was disassembled into 700 wooden segments; over 9,000 units of brick, tile or stone; and numerous items of daily necessity. These pieces filled some 40 containers, which were then shipped to the U.S to be reassembled at the Peabody Essex Museum.

The reassembling project of the Yinyu Hall in America

The Moon Pond of Hongcun Village

The neighborhood where the museum is located had broadened its roads and relocated quite a few residents in anticipation of the arrival of Yinyu Hall. It took seven years and 125 million U.S dollars to dismantle and reassemble the house, an exemplary feat of Sino-U.S engineering collaboration. The Yinyu Hall with more than 200 years' history was resurrected on the other side of the ocean.

On June 21st 2003 the Yinyu Hall was officially open to the public. Huizhou people attending the opening ceremony were moved by what they saw, and the Americans attracted by its reputation were astounded. The hall became the biggest news in the area.

As an American columnist stood observing the Yinyu Hall, tears ran down her cheeks. Looking up at a skylight, she exclaimed, "Standing here I seem to be gazing at the sky in China all through its 5,000 years' history."

In fact, there was more astounding news that reached the ancient Huizhou villages than just the selection of Yinyu Hall. In 2000, Xidi Village and Hongcun Village became a part of World Cultural Heritage.

Created more than 800 years ago, Hongcun Village is home to the Wang family in Huizhou. It is said that the ancestors of the Wang's hired feng shui experts to plan the village layout carefully in order to ensure peace and prosperity for the family. It took them ten years to dig ponds and ditches in the village. Stream water from outside the village is channelled into each household by a ditch more than 400 meters in length. This cobweb water system not only facilitates villagers' life and work, but also earns the village reputation of "A Village in a Traditional Chinese Painting". A famous scholar said, "If you want to learn about ancient Chinese palaces, visit the Palace Museum; if you want to learn about ancient Chinese houses, visit Xidi."

The ceremony of fixing the roof beam

About twenty kilometers from Hongcun Village, Xidi Village was created more than 100 years earlier. At present there are over 120 well preserved houses dating back to the Ming and Qing Dynasties in the village.

Ancient architecture should be protected and the secrets of traditional crafts should be passed on from one generation to another—an inheritance for those who follow.

Countless old houses are scattered across the more than 5,000 villages in Huizhou. Unfortunately, some of them have collapsed over the years, and others have been torn apart.

A restoration project was launched on a vacant lot in downtown She County. Like the Yinyu Hall, some treasured old houses were also taken apart with care by craftsmen and reassembled to their original grandeur.

This cluster of more than forty old buildings taking up an area of 20,000 square meters became the Huizhou Museum of Architecture upon completion in 2007. Through them, visitors can get a view of how the wealthy Huizhou merchants in the past illustrated the exquisite charm of Huizhou culture.

Tang Xianzu, a Ming Dynasty dramatist, once wrote, "Huizhou, a dreamland." Later generations may have different interpretations of what he meant, but his dream did start in the exquisite courtyards of Huizhou.

Chapter Twenty-One
Unnamed Shape of Huangshan

The sunrise at Huangshan Mountain

The ancient Western Path of Huangshan Mountain is less than two meters in width and twenty kilometers in length, but has been in existence in an obscure valley for more than 600 years.

In the past, since Huangshan was hardly accessible by land, people built this path adjacent to the Yangtze River. It might be a shortcut taken by ancient visitors to Huangshan, as it leads up to a hilltop where one can gaze back to the Yangtze River on one side and forward to Huangshan proper on the other. Any tour of Huangshan usually started with this mountain path that seemed to stretch endlessly ahead.

Huangshan began to attract people's attention more than 1,000 years after the Five Famous Mountains in China became well known during the reign of Emperor Wu of the Han Dynasty.

Popular opinion has it that Huangshan is just as majestic as Mount Tai, as misty as Mount Heng, with waterfalls comparable to those at Lushan and rocks as spectacular as those at Yandang Mountain. One might well say the Huangshan Mountain can't be named for an identifiable formation because all the various beautiful sceneries of other mountains can be found here.

Huangshan gained attention from the day when it assumed its current name. In the very beginning locals called Huangshan Mount Yi. It was said that Emperor Xuanzong of the Dang Dynasty renamed Mount Yi Huangshan in 747 after reading a legend in *Extraordinary Stories in the Zhou Dynasty* that Huangdi (or the Yellow Emperor, legendary ruler and ancestor of the Chinese nation) gathered herbs to make pills of immortality at Mount Yi south of the Yangtze River and finally ascended to Heaven. Huangshan means "Huangdi's mountain" in Chinese.

The Huangshan visited by tourists today is only a small portion of the entire range of the Huangshan Mountains.

Located in south Anhui Province, the Huangshan Mountains stretch a distance of over forty kilometers north to the south and about thirty kilometers east to the west. They borders with Tianmu Mountain to the east, Jiangxi Province to the southwest, Jiuhua Mountain to the north, and the Tunxi Basin to the south. The 154-square-kilometer Huangshan Scenic Area is a pick basket of natural beauty covering 1,200 square kilometers.

If you had never visited the mountain, it would be beyond imagination that people would queue up just to take a souvenir picture. One such site is in front of the thousand-year-old Guest Greeting Pine on top of the Bodhisattva Manjusri Cave east of the Jade Screen Peak. In the late 1950s, an iron picture depicting the tree was hung in the Anhui Room of the Great Hall of the People. Ever since then, the Guest Greeting Pine has been a symbol of Huangshan.

Pines on Huangshan were mentioned in books as early as the Song Dynasty. This species of pine unique to Huangshan got its unforgettable name, Huangshan Pine, in 1936 from botanist Xia Weiying.

Most Huangshan pines grow 800 meters above sea level out of cracks of apparently barren granite, which is in fact, rich in nutrients essential to the plants. They settle down in agreeable cracks on hilltops or cliff faces. The harsh environment forces them to grow at an extremely slow speed,

Huangshan pines

The sea of clouds at Huangshan Mountain

and to develop extensive root systems to grab nutrients from a wider area in order to survive. The roots of some ancient pines are several times, even dozens of times, the length of the trunks; a factor critical to life in these dire circumstances.

Tourists may find it unheard of that an ancient pine is being cared after twenty-four hours a day like a child or a senior citizen, but caretakers were assigned to the 1,300-year-old, ten-meter-tall Guest Greeting Pine over twenty years ago after a great snowstorm when stakes were used to support one of the side branches. Since the weather is changing all the time, they have to monitor closely the environment in which the treasured Guest Greeting Pine is growing and record any minor changes in great detail.

Caretakers have written over 6,000 diary entries such as this one:

"Wind force 5-6 last night. In good condition on both rounds. Heavy fog early in the morning, quite heavy dew. Many tourists in the morning."

Huangshan pines usually stand alone on mountain peaks but form forests in the lower cols. The abundant rainfall on Huangshan is soaked up by withered branches and dead leaves on the ground and then filter underground. Ground water in turn provides plants with adequate moisture which later evaporates into the air through roots, trunks and leaves. All these are conducive to the formation of the sea of clouds.

The cliff engravings

Grass rustles in the wind, heralding a mountain rain. Scenery at Huangshan often changes as the wind rises. When wind rises from down below, clouds will roll above the hills.

The meandering Huangshan Mountains with criss-crossing gullies span several climate zones ranging from the sub tropic zone to the cool temperate zone, again conducive to the development of clouds and fog.

The sea of clouds at Huangshan dwarfs that of other mountains by emerging more than 250 days out of a year. Some people have a different idea that the sea of clouds results from the forests. Strands of light fog are often seen rising from the deep valleys overgrown with trees, later forming into clouds. As the wind shifts the clouds may spiral up or dive down. The spectacular sea of clouds at Huangshan makes it all the more difficult to put your finger on the exact shape of Huangshan.

On one afternoon in May 1990, a Swiss man completed his long journey to Huangshan. He was Dr. Jim Sorsell, an expert from UNESCO. Upon his first view of the largest cliff engravings on Huangshan, he was lost in thought for a full fifteen minutes. He had come because Huangshan had applied to be a World Natural Heritage Site, but the same night he shocked authorities in Huangzhan by suggesting that "Huangshan should apply to become not only a World Natural Heritage Site, but also a World Cultural Heritage Site."

Well travelled as he was, Dr. Sorsell was impressed by what he saw on Huangshan, "Huangshan is the most unusual and wonderful among all the mountains I have seen." A few months later, on December 7th 1990, Huangshan became the only site approved by the 14th World Heritage Conference as both a World Cultural destination and a World Natural destination.

In the eyes of tourists "there are exotic rocks on all the peaks" of

"A Monkey Gazing at the Sea"

Huangshan, but in the eyes of scientists each stone, or even a light scratch on the rock surface, decodes some important message from antiquity.

Landscape on Huangshan in times of antiquity was not as majestic as it is now. It was through the polishing of such elements of nature as wind, rain, snow, frost and running water that the hard granite gradually took on its distinctly charming look. On Huangshan there are more than 120 named rocks like "A Monkey Gazing at the Sea". Those lifelike rocks would assume different appearances in different weather and it is always said that, "ridges or peaks, Huangshan look different from different perspectives."

Where there is a hill, there is water. "After a night's rain, waterfalls are everywhere in the mountain," what a proper description of springs and waterfalls on Huangshan!

Refreshed by torrential waterfalls, tireless streams, gurgling hot springs and serene ponds, Huangshan is all the more beautiful.

Xu Xiake, a Ming Dynasty geographer who visited Huangshan in winter

Dr. Jim Sorsell (the 4th on the left of the 2nd low), an expert from UNESCO was observing Huangshan Mountain in 1990.

The Shixing Peak of Huangshan Mountain painted by Jian Jiang (1610 - 1664), a famous Buddhist monk painter

1616, regarded his experience there as most unusual. Once asked by a friend wondering which was the most magical of all places he had visited, he answered, "I stopped admiring other mountains after my trip to Huangshan!" Later people turned his answer into a household saying: "You have no wish to visit any other mountains after visiting the Five Famous Mountains in China, and you don't even wish to visit the latter after you come back from Huangshan."

Researchers have confirmed that except for a small portion which flows into the Xin'an River and then into the Qiantang River, the majority of water from Huangshan's springs and waterfalls converges in the Taiping Lake at the foot of Huangshan and then empties into the Qingyi River which is connected to the Yangtze River. One may well say that Huangshan is a major water source for both the Qiantang River and the Yangtze River.

Streams meander through the Huangshan Mountains towards the embracing arms of the Yangtze River in the distance.

The fossil of the bowl-shaped ice of the Fourth Ice Age

The Jadeite Lake

Chapter Twenty-Two
Nanjing, the Stone City

The residential houses along the city walls

Nanjing is a city with 2,400 years' history on the Yangtze River.

There is a lantern show at the Confucian Temple on the bank of the Qinhuai River every Lantern Festival. Lantern makers are busy with their annual peak season as soon as the flood season of the Yangtze River is over. This year they will be able to sell more lotus lanterns because the Qinhuai Lantern Show event itself has become one of the first National Non-Material Cultural Heritages.

Many Nanjing residents have grown up near the city walls. Their life and fate are more or less connected to the wall as each brick of the city walls is marked with the names of the place where the brick was baked and the official in charge of that batch. An analysis of their rubbings revealed that all bricks had been made by mixing earth on either bank of the Yangtze River with water from the Yangtze River. Baked in kilns alongside the river, the bricks were then shipped over the river to Nanjing. Whether mixing or baking, shipping or building, many families lived their lives and owed their livelihood to the existence of the wall itself.

Nanjing is at the center of the lower section of the Yangtze River, which flows along its northwest side. To its east lies the 448.9-meter high Zhongshan Mountain (means Bell Mountain), also known as the Purple Mountain. To

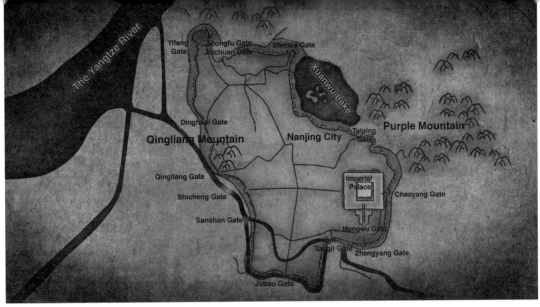

Sketch map of Nanjing city

its west lies the 63.7-meter Qingliang Mountain, also known as the "Stone Mountain". Since the Bell mountain resembles a coiling dragon in shape, and the Stone Mountain looks like a crouching tiger, Nanjing is said to be a forbidding strategic point.

The Purple Mountain provides natural protection for the plain in the lower reaches of the Yangtze River. About 2,400 years ago King Goujian of the Yue Kingdom built the city of Yue here. During the Three Kingdoms period Sun Quan built the Stone City on Qingliang Mountain. The succeeding East Jin, Song, Qi, Liang, and Chen Dynasties made it the capital, hence Nanjing's alias "Capital of Six Dynasties". It is a pity that nothing remains of the ancient capital. The city walls seen today were built upon orders from Zhu Yuanzhang, the First Emperor of the Ming Dynasty, whose management of state affairs was commended by Emperor Kangxi of the Qing Dynasty as "comparable to that of peak periods in the Tang and Song Dynasties".

Rubbing the characters on the bricks of the city walls

The bricks of the city walls

The sculpture of the Goddess Tianfei

The Lion Mountain lies near the Nanjing section of the Yangtze River. Zhu Yuanzhang once ordered the construction of the River Viewing Pavilion on its top. He not only wrote *Note on the River Viewing Pavilion* himself, but also asked each of his courtiers to write an essay. The one written by Imperial Secretary Song Lian found its way into *Anthology of Classical Prose*. The two essays survived the pavilion. It was not until 2001, more than 600 years after the destruction of the original pavilion, that the Xiaguan District Government had a new pavilion built. Both essays were inscribed onto stone tablets and placed there.

On top of the Lion Mountain two clusters of buildings are clearly visible at its foot- the Tianfei Palace and the Jinghai Temple. The Tianfei Palace was built in early Ming Dynasty upon orders from Emperor Yongle after he had heard from Zheng He, or Cheng Ho, his envoy to the West, how Goddess Tianfei helped his fleet survive storms on the sea. The Emperor also bestowed a stone tablet with his own inscriptions.

The Tianfei Palace was destroyed during the reign of Emperor Xianfeng of the Qing Dynasty and rebuilt in 2005. The tablet with imperial inscriptions is now kept at the Jinhai Temple constructed five years ahead of the Tianfei Palace.

Emperor Yongle had the Jinghai Temple built to grow exotic plants and store treasures brought back by Zheng He from overseas. "Jinhai" means "serene sea" in Chinese.

Serenity was broken some 400 years later in 1842, when the Qing Dynasty government, defeated in the Opium War, negotiated peace with British forces at the temple and then signed the Treaty of Nanjing, which humiliated the nation and forfeited its sovereignty, aboard the British warship HMS Cornwallis. Destroyed to a large extent in the end of the Qing Dynasty and during the Japanese occupation in the War of Resistance against Japanese Aggression, the Jinhai Temple has been restored in the past twenty years or so.

The history of Nanjing is embedded in the Ming Dynasty city walls. Children of Nanjing can't grow up without having a deep understanding of it.

Within the confines of Nanjing there are far more historic ruins left by war and disasters than the Tianfei Palace and the Jinghai Temple. The Ming Dynasty Imperial Palace built by Zhu Yuanzhang, which matched in size and grandeur with the Forbidden City in Beijing, was destroyed in the war at the end of the Qing Dynasty.

Following the example of Zhu Yuanzhang, Dr. Sun Yat-sen turned Nanjing into China's political center a second time. He took the oath of provisional President of the Republic of China in a house here in 1912, where he also promulgated over thirty statutes to establish the republic system.

Dr. Sun Yat-sen died in Beijing in 1925 and was buried at the Dr. Sun Yat-sen Mausoleum south of the Purple Mountain. He once predicted that "Nanjing has infinite potential of growth." He looked forward to a day when the city and the country could shake off tribulation and humiliation.

In front of his burial place lies the Fraternity Square. However, eight years later, instead of fraternity, the city of Nanjing was subject to the most atrocious brutality of the 20th century.

In December 1937, the invading Japanese army seized Nanjing and started a wave of ruthless killing. According to statistics publicized by the 1947 War

The former site of the Presidential Palace

The Fraternity Square of the Dr. Sun Yat-sen Mausoleum

The Memorial Hall for Compatriots Killed in the Nanjing Massacre by Japanese Forces of Aggression

Crimes Tribunal, Japanese invaders killed more than 300,000 civilians and soldiers unfit for fighting in Nanjing. The Memorial Hall for Compatriots Killed in the Nanjing Massacre by Japanese Forces of Aggression, established in 1985, has become a place for people to mourn for Nanjing's victims and to pray for peace. It also conveys a message to Nanjing's children: Nanjing has not been beaten by all the trials and tribulations.

On December 13th 2005, on the 68th remembrance of the Nanjing Massacre, piercing sirens were heard all over Nanjing.

The Chinese of past ages dreamed of spanning the chasm posed by the Yangtze River to Nanjing. It is extremely difficult to build a bridge over the great river here at Nanjing, because by this time the east-bound river has claimed a much wider course with a maximum breadth of 2.5 kilometers and a minimum of 1.5 kilometers.

On May 22nd 2005, the two sections of China's first steel tower, cable bridge over the Yangtze River were joined. Measuring 15.6 kilometers in length, it is Nanjing's third bridge over the Yangtze River; 19 kilometers upstream from the Nanjing Yangtze River Bridge constructed 37 years before.

It was a major event for the newly established People's Republic of China to finish the surveying and construction of the Nanjing Yangtze River Bridge in eight years. On December 29th 1968, when trains and automobiles appeared on the bridge all designed and built by Chinese hands, the whole nation was jubilant. The north-south artery road across the lower reaches of the Yangtze River was successfully linked.

In March 2001, a cable bridge appeared across the Nanjing section of the Yangtze River. Local residents called it the Second Bridge.

The world's first arc steel tower cable bridge, the Third Nanjing Yangtze River Bridge, is lit up by over 700 lamps and over 2000 suites of nightscape illumination.

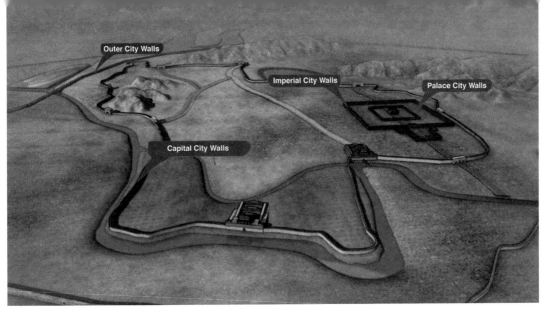
Sketch map of Nanjing city walls

Echoing the lightings on the Yangtze River bridges are the multi-colored lights in the city of Nanjing; radiating warmth and reassurance to local residents. Moreover, for those wishing for greater assurance, China's largest copper cast Bixie, a mythical beast said to be able to ward off evil spirits, is standing on guard outside the city's Zhongshan Gate.

Zhu Yuanzhang had four rings of city walls built in Nanjing: the one around his palaces was located in the east of the city and had a circumference of 3.4 kilometers; a second ring for the imperial city, which included the palaces, had a length of 2.5 kilometers north to south, a width of 2 kilometers east to west and a total circumference of 8.23 kilometers; the third wall for the capital, with a total of 13 city gates, had a length of 35.267 kilometers; and finally, the 60-kilometer wall of the outer city with its 18 gates.

Of all 13 ancient city gates in Nanjing, the Shence Gate restored in the Qing Dynasty is the only one which could be seen with a gate tower. Sections of the city walls have been destroyed by wars or erosion in 600 years' time. By the end of 1958, about one third of the city walls had been demolished. According to surveys done by the Nanjing Municipal Bureau for the Preservation of Cultural and Historical Relics in 2006, the existing city walls above ground have a total length of 25.091 kilometers, still the longest among all ancient city walls still in existence today.

The Ming Dynasty city walls in Nanjing became an Important Heritage Site under State Protection in 1988, which triggered the restoration and cleanup efforts in Nanjing, and the formulation of the 1992 Master Plan for

The Xuanwu Gate

the Scenery along the Ming Dynasty city walls in Nanjing. In early 2005 the Nanjing Municipal Government began to clean up the area inside 1.5-kilometer section of the city walls between the Xuanwu Gate and the Jiefang Gate. According to their plans some 1,032 households were to be relocated.

About 80% of the remnant city walls in Nanjing were restored between 1988 and the end of 2005, and 90% of the area around the walls were cleaned up. Other important cultural relics in Nanjing have also received protection, restoration or reconstruction. The Cockcrow Temple dating back to the Ming Dynasty has become the most popular temple in Nanjing since its reconstruction in 1979.

The Jiangnan Imperial Examination Center, the largest of its kind in the Qing Dynasty, is now home to the country's only exhibition on the history of imperial examinations.

The Dacheng Hall of the Confucian Temple destroyed seven times since the initial construction in the North Song Dynasty, has become one of the most important scenic spots in Nanjing after its reconstruction in 1986.

Protected or reconstructed, these

The Peace Gate

The Confucian Temple in Nanjing

sites of cultural and historical interests are not only part of the cultural heritage in this former imperial capital on the river, but also tourist destinations spurring on the city's growth and development.

The new Nanjing Library stands tall and erect across from the former Presidential Palace. During its construction, researchers from the Nanjing Museum, armed with knowledge of Nanjing and historical data, seized chances to conduct archaeological excavations. They found a well and a section of city walls buried five meters underground. Both dating back to the Six Dynasties, they provided a peek into the ancient capital.

As the ancient Nanjing city undergoes renovations it is also more and more modernized. The Jinling Hotel at Xinjiekou doesn't look quite impressive today, but it used to be the landmark of Nanjing.

Renovated city walls and the areas nearby have become ideal places of morning exercises and recreation for Nanjing residents.

After years of efforts, areas around city walls at Xiaotaoyuan, the Jiqing Gate, the Qingliang Gate, the Xuanwu Lake and the Shence Gate have become scenic spots.

The Qinhuai River is the Mother River to Nanjing. A tributary of the Yangtze River, the Qinhuai flows from the southeast of the city, girdles half of it, and then joins the Yangtze River. When Zhu Yuanzhang had the city of Nanjing built, he also ordered the construction of a distribution channel to

The night sceneries on the Qinhuai River

divide the river into Inner and Outer Qinhuai.

The cleaned up Outer Qinhuai and the Inner Qinhuai flank the Ming Dynasty city walls for over 20 kilometers. Beautiful as they are, they add a touch of gentleness to this solemn former imperial city on the Yangtze River.

The Inner Qinhuai has been a favorite topic for the literati for hundreds of years. The annual lantern show which lights it has made a name for itself too.

Each year, as the last month on the Chinese lunar calendar draws to a close, a market for selling and enjoying lanterns opens. As the days go by more and more people come here to buy or sell lanterns until a climax is reached on the 15th day of the first month on the Chinese lunar calendar. It has long been a custom in Nanjing to hold lantern shows in times of prosperity. In times of turbulence lantern shows were discontinued.

According to historical annals the lantern show on the Qinhuai River started in the Six Dynasties and peaked in the Ming and Qing Dynasties. Legend has it that on the Lantern Festival during the fifth year of his reign, Emperor Hongwu, or Zhu Yuanzhang, ordered the display of ten thousand lanterns on the river, a sight so spectacular that one almost suspected that the Milky Way had descended on earth.

The annual lantern show was resumed in Nanjing in 1985. Every year in the past three years, over 300,000 people spent a festive Lantern Festival night at the Confucian Temple lantern show.

The Qinhuai River becomes a dreamland of rowing boats and lanterns, and visitors are welcoming the return of its splendour.

Chapter Twenty-Three
The Yangtze River Delta

The eastbound Yangtze River flows in a much wider course in the lower reaches. With an annual flow of close to one trillion cubic meters, it can welcome more ships than the upper and middle reaches.

Near the confluence point between the Yangtze River and the East China Sea, a fan-shaped plain has been created by the sedimentation of sand in the Yangtze River, otherwise known as a delta. Covering an area of about 40,000 square kilometers, the Yangtze River Delta is China's largest estuary delta.

Abundant water in the river nurtured early settlers on the Yangtze River Delta, where rice grown 7,000 years ago has been found. Ever since then, the agricultural society and economy has been developing on this land richly endowed by nature.

Agricultural progress provided opportunities and momentum to the development of the handicraft industry in the Yangtze River Delta. More than 6,000 years ago people living here used their hands to make practical tools like ploughs out of animal bones. Later they came up with techniques to make pottery, build wooden and earthen houses, and weave silk and cloth. These products promoted trade which in turn further stimulated agriculture. As a result of the sustained agriculture and the means of transporting goods, the Yangtze River Delta has always been the wealthiest region in China.

The handicraft industry in the Yangtze River Delta thrived for several

The Panmen Gate of Suzhou

thousand years. Close to both the Yangtze River and the sea, it has seized the latest opportunity to develop itself into China's largest manufacturing base.

Suzhou, a renowned Paradise on Earth with over 2,500 years' history, is located in central Yangtze River Delta. Back in time ingenious city designers built a city on water to take advantage of abundant water resources in the Yangtze River and the Tai Lake. It was typical of the city and of its residents to integrate water into diversified spatial layouts. Due to such ingenuity Suzhou has become a beautiful and innovative city in the Yangtze River Delta for the past twenty years.

There is a well preserved ancient city gate in Suzhou so cleverly designed that is accessible by both land and water. As late as twenty years ago cargo freight ships still travelled on rivers in Suzhou. However, with the development of the infrastructure for road transportation, all rivers except for the Great Canal, together with this 2,500-year-old Panmen Gate, have become tourist attractions of the city.

Like their ancestors, Suzhou residents today have a temperament as nimble as the water. Tourism used to be Suzhou's pillar industry. Tourists from all over the country came to see with their own eyes the famous gardens in Suzhou.

The acronym Su-Xi-Chang refers to three cities in central Yangtze River Delta that are kilometers apart from each other: Suzhou, Wuxi and Changzhou. The acronym came into being twenty years ago when the economy in these three cities began to take off. At present they are the most economically active cities in the entire Yangtze River Basin and even the entire country, boasting six counties out of the 2005 Top Ten Economic Powerhouse Counties in China.

In 1999, 62 years after the completion of the Golden Gate Bridge in San Francisco, the world's first large-span suspension bridge, a suspension bridge whose length ranks number one in China and number four in the world was drawn across the Yangtze River at Jiangyin. Two cables 2,178 meters in length and 8,390 tons in weight suspend the bridge.

After that a metal "monument"

The steel wires

The Runyang Bridge on the Yangtze River

sprung up at the riverside park nearby. Consisting of over 20,000 lengths of endless steel wire 3.5 mm in diameter, it is actually a cable identical to the two suspension cables on the bridge. Made in Jiangyin, the gigantic steel wire has become a legend in its own right.

A rope-making factory of 54 employees forty years earlier has now been magically transformed into one of the world's largest cable manufacturers; its products have evolved from natural fiber ropes to bridge cables and then on to optical fibers.

For the past twenty years innovation has been behind the economic takeoff of the Yangtze River Delta. Over 200,000 workers are busy at assembly lines every day at the Suzhou Industrial Park. These modern workshops were built on former farmland, and the high-tech products they turn out are sold around the world.

Located beside the Jinji Lake in east Suzhou, the Suzhou Industrial Park covers an area of 282 square kilometers. The long history of manufacturing in the Yangtze River Delta convinced the Chinese and Singaporean Governments to locate their first joint industrial park here in Suzhou. The resulting project has become one of the most competitive development zones in Asia, attracting 53 of the world's top 500 companies to set up facilities here by the end of 2005.

Kunshan, a neighbor of Shanghai's, is an example of a city that has undertaken the most transformation in the Yangtze River Delta; well illustrated by the change in its total economic output from a mere RMB 576 million in

Workshop of the Suzhou Industrial Park

1984 to RMB 73 billion in 2005. At present it ranks Number 1 in the listing of top 100 Economic Powerhouse Counties in China.

Many foreign companies, and even more importantly, companies from Taiwan have placed their facilities in Kunshan, giving economy in Kunshan a great boost. The IT industry has become a major pillar for the Kunshan Development Zone. At least twenty of the top 500 companies in the world have a presence here, as do six out of the ten major notebook computer manufacturers based in Taiwan. In 2005, Kunshan produced 7.5 million digital cameras and 15.25 million notebook computers, approximately one third of the world's total output.

The manufacturing industry prospers in the Yangtze River Delta because of its rich heritage: skilful craftsmen have always gathered here from old times, and rope-driven looms here used to weave the most gorgeous silk on earth.

The Forbidden City was paved with bricks baked in Suzhou; purchased and ordered by Kuai Xiang, Supervisor General of the construction of the Forbidden City, a native from Suzhou.

Consummate skills passed down from generation to generation crystallize creativity on this land as well as the wisdom of its inhabitants. With time passing by many traditional manufacturing techniques are now only seen in museums, but the innovative spirit in the Yangtze River Delta is as inexhaustible as the rushing torrents in the Yangtze River.

Record has it that the Yangtze River joined the sea at Jiangyin more than 2,000 years ago. There is a stone tablet at Jiangyin's Ebizui Park on the bank of the Yangtze River, whose inscriptions read, "Tail of River, and Head of Sea."

If, metaphorically speaking, the manufacturing industry in the Yangtze River Delta has developed from a trickle to a river of roaring waves; it is now at the tail of the river and at the head of the sea. After years of growth it is ready to face the immense ocean of economic globalization.

Chapter Twenty-Four
Suzhou on Rivers

Kunqu, one of China's oldest traditional operas, has been in existence for more than 600 years, although only over 200 of the original 1,800-plus scenes have been preserved.

A *qinggong* in Kunqu who specializes in the singing but not the spoken parts of any Kunqu opera is simply referred to as a "singer".

There are usually 30 to 50 scenes in a complete Kunqu drama. A Kunqu school is supposed to not only keep the lyrics and music scores of each scene, but also teach the most authentic way of oral delivery. Sometimes the "singers" are more particular about oral delivery than professional actors and actresses. They tape record everything in a performance, creating an audio treasury of the ancient Kunqu.

The Suzhou Kunqu school

When an old man hummed a tune in his vine-covered courtyard, passers-by wouldn't pay much attention, because to Suzhou residents Kunqu has always been a part of their life.

The best sceneries in Suzhou are concealed beyond creeks and bridges in gardens scattering all around the city.

Few could actually build a garden, but many Suzhou residents dream of doing so. If the city of Suzhou resembles a large garden of "bridges, running water and houses", then an ordinary household in Suzhou is comparable to a scaled-down garden. Inside an inconspicuous gate there might be some

The Shantang Street

scenery of exceptional charm. In courtyards large or small, there are always a couple of bonsais, several kinds of flowers, and a miniature pond despite the fact that Suzhou is already a city on rivers.

The Shantang Street outside the ancient city walls came into being more than 1,100 years ago, whereas the ancient Suzhou city has existed more than 2,500 years. Legend has it that Wu Zixu built this city of eight gates in 514 B.C., and that garden building activities in the city started 100 years later. According to historical data the number of gardens in Suzhou throughout its history exceeds 1,000. They were all designed to imitate nature.

The Panmen Gate, whose initial construction started in 512 B.C., is one of the eight city gates in Suzhou, and also the only ancient city gate still intact and accessible by both land and water in the world.

Cui Yuan (Green Garden)

The Cang Lang Ting (The Surging Wave Pavilion)

A quote from one poem has become just one of the many coined phrases that speak of the deep attachment people here have to their river, their gardens and the outlying areas: "Outside Suzhou Hanshan Temple is in sight; its ringing bells reach my boat at midnight." Nourished by the Yangtze River, Suzhou has expanded from an ancient city of "manmade gardens within city confines" to a modern "garden city surrounded by real hills and real rivers".

In 2004, Suzhou became the first Chinese city to host a session of the World Heritage Committee on the strength of its gardens, which are World Heritage sites, Kunqu, a Non Material Cultural Heritage, and the right balance between history and modernity.

Girdled by blue water, Cang Lang Ting dating back to 1041 is the oldest existing garden in Suzhou. Its first owner was Su Shunqin, a government official during the reign of Emperor Qingli of the North Song Dynasty. It was said that he bought the garden and named it Cang Lang Ting after suffering setbacks in his political career.

About 500 years after the completion of Cang Lang Ting, another frustrated government official Wang Xianchen retired to Suzhou from his position as Supervisor of Offical Conduct. It took him four years to build the Humble Administrator's Garden, the largest garden in Suzhou covering an area of more than 200 *mu*. In his time landscape designing was all the rage, as was Kunqu.

Within the Humble Administrator's Garden there is a special venue for

The stage inside the Humble Administrator's Garden

the owner to enjoy Kunqu, receive guests and admire mandarin ducks playing on water—the Thirty-Six Mandarin Duck Mansion, where the roof comprises four successive arches that both please the eyes and enhance the acoustic effect. For more than 400 years since its completion, the Humble Administrator's Garden has seen its owners and guests sitting in verandas facing each other, enjoying water lilies, observing fish and the lingering notes of Kunqu.

Melodious Kunqu is heard on stages put up in gardens. During the 400 years' time when the gardens and Kunqu complimented each other perfectly in Suzhou, the city's economy also experienced an unparalleled boom.

A renowned "Paradise on Earth", half the area of Suzhou is taken up by water supplied by rivers, lakes and tributaries in the Yangtze River Delta. With such plentiful water, this may be the only place where the construction of so many gardens is feasible, and where the painstakingly tender Kunqu, the forerunner of all traditional Chinese operas, could arise.

In the late Yuan Dynasty and early Ming Dynasty, Gu Jian, who gave himself another name "A Specialist in Wind and Moon", composed poetry to chant with friends at his home in Shiban Street, Qiandeng Town, Kunshan County of Suzhou. As time passed, the Kunshan Tune became very well known. During the reign of Emperor Jiajing of the Ming Dynasty, Wei Liangfu, a temperament expert, combined Kunshan Tune with the then popular Yuyao and Haiyan Tunes as well as other tunes heard south of the Yangtze River to form Kunqu, which prevailed in the following 200-plus years.

Kunqu not only boasts a long history, but also a rich repertoire integrating poetry, music, singing and dancing. It epitomizes traditional operas in China.

Over the 200-plus years Kunqu spread widely throughout the Yangtze River Basin via the Yangtze River, leaving great impact on such subsequent operas as Peking opera, Shaoxing opera and Sichuan opera, hence Kunqu's reputation as

The Hu Qiu (Tiger Hill)

forerunner of all traditional Chinese operas.

There is a huge rock, nicknamed "Thousand Persons' Rock", at the foot of Hu Qiu northwest of Suzhou. The largest natural stage in Suzhou, it was an important venue for Kunqu performances when Kunqu was received enthusiastically.

The plebeian class emerging in the late Qing Dynasty was averse to the slow melancholic Kunqu. Despite having such a grand stage of its own, Kunqu gradually became obsolete.

According to records, on Mid Autumn Festival every year, Suzhou residents gathered at Hu Qiu to perform Kunqu while enjoying the round bright moon. On such highly festive occasions, one could hardly tell performance artists from members of the audience.

The hill was named Hu Qiu 2,500 years ago. Throughout history it has always been as famous as the gardens in Suzhou, since it is as old as the city itself.

In 1997, four gardens in Suzhou became UNESCO's World Cultural and Natural Heritage sites. In 2000, five other gardens in Suzhou applied to become World Heritage sites, among which the Retreat and Meditation Garden

The Lion Forest Garden

in Tongli Town, Suzhou is the best known.

The Retreat and Meditation Garden was built by Ren Lansheng, a dismissed government official during the reign of Emperor Guangxu of the Qing Dynasty at a cost of 100,000 taels of silver. The name of the garden was derived from the saying of "be loyal when in office and meditate on mistakes when out of office".

Large or small, the classical gardens scattering around Suzhou are masterpieces by skilful Suzhou craftsmen over 2,000 years. However, being created for retiring administrators and locals, these gardens are dwarfed by what the same craftsmen have achieved in the Ming Dynasty Imperial Palace in Nanjing and the Forbidden City in Beijing.

Lion Forest Garden got its name from the many lion-like Taihu Lake Stones found in it.

The teahouse in the garden is frequented by senior residents of Suzhou fond of Kunqu and gardens. Invariably they come to chat at the teahouse, and invariably they chat about gardens. They are very familiar with the story of the garden they are in.

The last owner of Lion Forest

The Retreat and Meditation Garden

The teahouse in the Lion Forest Garden

Garden is surnamed Bei. The world-class architect and mastermind behind the Suzhou Museum, I.M.Pei (a.k.a. Bei), grew up in this garden.

As a result of wars and disturbances, only 69 classical gardens remain in Suzhou. In 1992, Suzhou led the way in the country by writing the protection of classical gardens into local rules and regulations.

Built during the reign of Emperor Tongzhi of late Qing Dynasty, Yi Garden is the youngest private gardens in Suzhou. It is a collection of fine landscape designs from all other gardens.

On May 18th 2001 UNESCO included Kunqu in the first list of "Masterpieces of Oral and Intangible Heritage of Humanity."

To Suzhou residents Kunqu and gardens are in the same tradition, the former full of audio turns and twists, the latter full of spatial turns and twists. To them gardens are Kunqu in its visible form, and Kunqu is gardens in their audible form. After Kunqu became a World Heritage, Kunqu performances resumed on the stage in Wangshi Yuan (the Master of the Nets), which had been deserted for quite some time.

In 1993, construction began on a gigantic garden which occupies an area of over 100 *mu* in the ancient town of Tongli, home to the Retreat and Meditation Garden. However, instead of a retired government official, the owner of this garden is a Suzhou resident who made his fortune after China's

Jingsi Yuan (Calm and Meditation Garden) in Tongli

Reform and Opening Up and who is willing to spend all he has to realize his long-cherished dream of recreating classical Suzhou gardens which have left such indelible impressions on his young mind.

Jingsi Garden could be said to be home to the best sights in classical gardens south of the Yangtze River. In it there is a hall made of Phoebe nanmu wood dating back to the Ming Dynasty, a mahogany hall dating back to the Qing Dynasty, and a huge Lingbi stone several meters taller than the Guanyun Peak at Suzhou's Liu Garden.

Apart from ancient architecture, the owner takes great pride in his collection of ancient bridges. The over 100 bridges spanning the over 20 *mu* of water are the soul of his Jingsi Garden.

In the past, garden owners in Suzhou kept the garden, water lilies, running water and Kunqu to themselves and their honored guests. At present, the owner of Suzhou's largest newly built garden shares his garden and his dreams with all people who want to come and enjoy it.

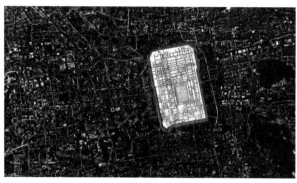

The satellite remote sensing map of Suzhou (highlighted is the ancient city of Pingjiang)

When comparing the oldest existent lithographic city map in the world with a contemporary satellite remote sensing city map, people were surprised to find that the general layout of this ancient city hadn't changed much during the 700-odd years. The city then known as Pingjiang now goes by the name of Suzhou.

Chapter Twenty-Five
Discovering Ancient Towns

Twenty years ago, painter Chen Yifei finished an oil painting entitled *Memory of Hometown* in which he depicted two connected stone bridges, known to locals as Twin Bridges. In 1985 Dr. Armand Hammer presented this painting in his collection to Deng Xiaoping. The Twin Bridges have made Zhouzhuang famous.

Dr. Armand Hammer presented the painting *Memory of Hometown* to Deng Xiaoping in 1985.

Today, Zhouzhuang of Kunshan County, Suzhou, an ancient town of "small bridges, streams and houses" established more than 900 years ago, is regarded by critics as a model of "well-preserved water town south of the Yangtze River".

The Jishui Dock north of the 2.47-square-kilometer Zhouzhuang could be used to access the four provinces of Jiangsu, Zhejiang, Anhui and Jiangxi. According to *County Annals of Zhouzhuang*, the area started to prosper in the Ming Dynasty after the arrival of Shen Wansan, a wealthy merchant well known south of the Yangtze River.

In 1985, Prof. Ruan Yisan from the Department of Architecture at Tongji University happened to visit Zhouzhang, a forgotten town whose glory had faded away. Water transportation being its only link to the outside world, Zhouzhuang was isolated for lack of a highway much preferred by modern people. When Prof. Ruan from Shanghai arrived at Zhouzhuang after an entire day's journey, the ancient town was wrapped in night stillness.

The plan for Zhouzhuang by Prof. Ruan Yisan

Pictures taken by Prof. Ruan 20 years ago could help people imagine how serene and rustic Zhouzhuang was in its out-of-the-way days. Before his encounter with Zhouzhuang, Prof. Ruan had visited many other ancient towns south of the Yangtze River to explain the importance of cultural preservation. However back then, in their rush to make quick money, people were more enthusiastic about developing village and township enterprises than taking his advice.

It may have been destiny that saved Zhouzhuang for Ruan Yisan. During the two summer vacations in 1985 and 1986, Ruan Yisan surveyed the entire town of Zhouzhuang with the help of forty to fifty students from Tongji University's Department of Architecture. After returning to Tongji they recreated every river, old bridge and house at Zhouzhuang in ink and paper on the basis of survey data. This drawing may be the most comprehensive record of Zhouzhuang ever available in history.

In several months' time Ruan Yisan brought back to Zhouzhuang a drawing much simpler than the one depicting the status quo—the development plan for Zhouzhuang. On it were three circles defining the boundaries of the old town, the new town and the industrial area, respectively. The 0.47-square-kilometer old town was to be protected.

Thanks to that planning, all industrial development in the past 20 years has taken place outside of the old town. Zhouzhuang of old was preserved.

At that time many buildings in the ancient Zhouzhuang town were dilapidated. Not a single door, window pane, or tile was intact at the Shen Residence, a huge compound of over 100 rooms covering an area of 2,000 square meters. Once inhabited by the rich, well-known merchant from the south, Shen Wansan, the house symbolized the prosperity he and his family brought to Zhouzhuang.

In 1986, RMB 20,000 Yuan was allocated by the Provincial Department

The Twin Bridges in 1930

Zhouzhuang in 1985

of Culture to purchase and restore the Shen Residence. All houses built in the town in the same time period as the Shen Residence were researched in order to find out windows and doors appropriate for the Shen Residence. Eventually in a house next door a wooden window with carved Chinese flowering crab apple blossoms was found to date back to the same age as the Shen Residence.

In the following winter, old carpenters summoned from the neighboring countryside repaired all doors and windows at the Shen Residence by adopting the Chinese flowering crab apple blossom pattern. When spring arrived all restoration work at the Shen Residence had been done.

The Twin Bridges, which had brought prosperity back to Zhouzhuang, comprise a stone arch bridge and a stone beam bridge first built in the Ming Dynasty. The two bridges run perpendicular to each other, and the bridge openings are square and round respectively. Regarded together they resemble an ancient key, hence their other name "Key Bridge". Zhouzhuang residents still use the two bridges daily. Two entirely different proposals were made by experts before servicing the bridges in 1999.

After much consideration, it was decided that the two bridges should be restored without damaging the original look. Construction workers numbered each slab of stone as they disassembled entire bridges, built a steel-and-concrete version leaning towards the south as the original ones did, and then pasted the stone slabs onto the former. In half a year's time the reinforced Twin Bridges emerged as if nothing whatsoever had been changed to alter them.

In that year more than one million tourists walked on the Twin Bridges.

The Twin Bridges

In 2005, Zhouzhuang's tourism revenue climbed to RMB 780 million Yuan from 2.6 million tourists. Zhouzhuang residents profited handsomely from the more than 600 stores and businesses catering to tourists. Bustling at the Zhang Residence where "sedans passed by the gate and boats were rowed on premise", this water taxi service has been resumed and utilized by many people as well as the Zhang's.

Fu'an Bridge is located in front of the Shen Residence in central Zhouzhuang more than 100 meters south of Twin Bridges. It is the only existent architecture combining a bridge with towers among all water towns south of the Yangtze River. Before restoration its four towers were occupied by some rundown barber shops and a traditional Chinese pharmacy. In 1988 they were turned into four restaurants facing each other, where tourists could wine and dine while small boats passed leisurely under the bridge.

The short 100-meter-long stretch of river between Fu'an Bridge and Twin Bridges is the best water town scenery to be found in Zhouzhuang.

Towns south of the Yangtze River boomed in the Ming and Qing Dynasties. In the past centuries the cobweb Tai Lake water system has given birth to many wealthy water towns. Ten years after Zhouzhuang became a tourist destination, one ancient town after another revived itself to follow suit.

The One-Hundred-Room House may probably be the most typical water town architecture in existence south of the Yangtze River. In the Ming Dynasty, Dong Fen, a native of Nanxun Town, Huzhou of Zhejiang Province sailed

The One-Hundred-Room House in Nanxun Town

through Imperial Examinations first at the provincial level and then the national level, and went on to become Minister of Rites and Member of the Imperial Academy. In his old age he returned to his hometown, where he built more than 100 rooms opening onto streets on both the eastern and western banks of the old canal in Nanxun, hence the name "One-Hundred-Room" House.

The architectural style of the One-Hundred-Room House differs from that of typical water town houses such as those at Zhouzhuang. Unlike the "small bridges, streams and houses" of the latter, the rivers at Nanxun are wider and the stone bridges are taller.

Most people living at the One-Hundred-Room house right now are Nanxun natives, although it's unclear how many of them are related to the Dong family in the Ming Dynasty.

The inhabitants of the One-Hundred-Room House go on with their busy yet leisurely lives, the rain shelter along the river connecting one household to another.

The atmosphere at a much more prosperous residence on the other side of Nanxun feels totally different. The towering horse-head gable walls and spacious courtyards distinguish its owner from others.

In early 1994, the former residence of Zhang Jingjiang at the ancient Nanxun town was chosen as the first old house to be restored. He was a legendary figure in Nanxun: a famous Huzhou merchant, he made generous contributions to uprisings led by Dr. Sun Yat-sen.

A group photo of Dr. Sun Yat-sen (the 3rd on the left) and Zhang Jingjiang (the 3rd on the right)

Zhang Jingjiang

Nanxun natives compared the wealth of established families in town to the size of animals—there were "Four Elephants, Eight Bulls and 72 Golden Retrievers" in Nanxun. The Zhang family was one of the Four Elephants.

Their wealth could all be traced back to Jili Village of Nanxun. In 1852, Huzhou Silk produced at Jili won a gold prize at the First World Expo held in London. Thanks to the Changxing- Huzhou- Shanghai water route, silk dealers in Nanxun were able to cover all silk producers in Huzhou, which included Nanxun.

According to statistics collected by the Shanghai Customs, half of the silk stocks exported at the Shanghai Port between 1843 and 1848 were from Nanxun. And the clothes of the Qing Dynasty royal family had to be made from Huzhou silk. After making a fortune, Huzhou silk dealers at the time competed to build grand homes at Nanxun, their hometown. They were the so-called "Four Elephants, Eight Bulls and 72 Golden Retrievers", depending on their level wealth and influence.

One kilometer away from Zhang Jingjiang's house is the residence of his cousin Zhang Shiming, a huge cluster covering an area in Nanxun of over 5,000 square meters that has been fully restored.

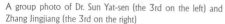

The former residence of Zhang Shiming

Zhang Shiming's mother's bedroom

On a Sunday in October 1996 a group of French tourists visited Zhang Shiming's residence right before the start of the restoration project. Something unexpected came into sight when they came to the bedroom of Zhang Shiming's mother on the second floor in a building in the inner courtyard.

It is probably the case that secrets are often uncovered by chance. More than two months later, those French wrote back from their own country, saying that only seven window panes processed

The custom-made glass from France in Zhang Shiming's mother's bedroom

with the same technique had been found by the French National Museum, and that the technique had been lost in France.

A colored floor tile in the last row of rooms at Zhang Shiming's residence gave the French yet another pleasant surprise. They said that such tiles with landscape oil paintings on them were rare in foreign countries too. Judging by the position of the colored floor tile and the flue nearby, they surmised the existence years before of a western-style fireplace. Later they sent a drawing explaining how and where the fireplace utensils should be placed.

When the fireplace and the entire hall had been restored, people had a clear picture of the magnificent ballroom once owned by Zhang Shiming's family in the ancient Nanxun town. When many Chinese men were still wearing pigtails and Chinese women still had their feet bound, the owners of this house were waltzing over a French mosaic floor.

The western-style building of Zhang Shiming's family in Nanxun

Outside the dancing hall one finds a combination of Chinese and Western landscaping: Roman columns and red brick walls are set off by huge magnolia trees, blue Chinese tiles top a European-style building. However, the tall horse-head gable walls surrounding the compound block everything Western from the view of outsiders. Maybe the more traditional-minded Chinese found it difficult to accept the better informed and better connected families in Nanxun; or maybe the oriental reserve was uncomfortable confronting the Western conspicuousness.

Xiaolianzhuang (Little Lotus Villa) is a garden estate built by the Liu's, the wealthiest of the "Four Elephants", during the reign of Emperor Guangxu of the Qing Dynasty. Close to the water lily pond stands a western-style building for the daughters as well as a family memorial archway.

When the silk stocks were transported in small boats from their doorsteps to Shanghai where it was loaded onto big ocean-going vessels, the houses in their hometown were more like hotels to them than real homes. Their offspring seemed to have failed to hold onto the family property and value it as well. The Nanxun silk merchants who used to have wealth worthy of a country's treasury have lost their significance as times changed. However, a haven for the mind created by them has survived.

Wu Town in Jiaxing, Zhejiang Province

In the ancient town of Nanxun there is a building undamaged by wars and turbulences—the Jiaye Cangshulou (Jiaye Private Library). It took Liu Chenggan, one of the later generations of the Liu's, 22 years and 120,000 taels of silver to build the largest library south of the Yangtze River, where over 10,000 block-printed editions and local annals from the Song, Ming and Qing Dynasties were preserved.

The majority of those rare books later found their way into major Chinese libraries. The rest are still in their old home in Nanxun.

The ancient towns south of the Yangtze were built along rivers, and stone arch bridges of different shapes integrated rivers well into roads.

Nowadays those ancient towns have become sites of cultural interest along the lower reaches of the Yangtze River. The number of tourists visiting Zhouzhuang every year has exceeded two million.

These ancient towns will remind us from time to time how our hometowns along the Yangtze River used to be.

The six most famous ancient towns along the Yangtze River

Chapter Twenty-Six
The Pace of Shanghai

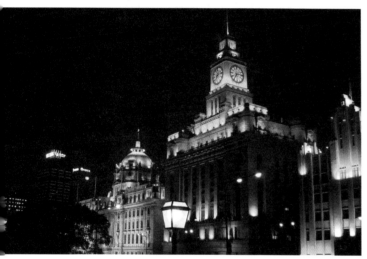
The Custom House

The centenarian city of Shanghai is the last metropolis along the Yangtze River before it joins the sea, also home to one of the first customs houses in China.

The Customs House has always been a landmark on the Bund in Shanghai. Its clock and bell has been chiming for over 110 years, a witness to life and changes in Shanghai over the century, and the aging of those buildings along the Bund, a walker's "Museum of International Architecture."

The earliest customs house, or Northern Jianghai Guan, was built in 1857. The second customs house, designed by the British, was completed in 1893 and carried a bell tower. A third customs house was built by the then National Government in 1927, on top of which sat the largest clock in Asia at the time. The clock was made in Britain and cost 2,000 taels of silver. With a 3.6-meter-long minute hand on each of the four 5.3-meter-diameter faces, Shanghai residents and visitors from all directions could keep up with the times.

After 1949 the Shanghai Customs kept the building but changed the clock and bell in several ways. When the building was completed Westminster was played on the quarter hour. During the Cultural Revolution the clock face was covered with sunflower patterns and the melody was changed to The East Is Red.

The frescos on the dome in the lobby of Shanghai Pudong Development Bank

In 1984 the melody was switched back to the British tune and the sunflower patterns were removed. Before Hong Kong's return to Chinese sovereignty, the clock and bell again played The East Is Red.

Roles played by buildings on the Bund changed several times as well. Next door to the Customs house is the former HSBC building completed in 1923. Shanghai Municipal Government moved into it in 1955, turning the Bund into the political center of Shanghai.

In 1995, Shanghai Municipal Government moved to a new site on the People's Square. Shanghai Pudong Development Bank became the new proud owner of this building. Accounts record that its initial construction cost is said to account for half of the total cost of all building activities on the Bund within the same time period, so much so that the British regarded it as the most luxurious building between the Suez Canal and the Bering Strait.

The eight mosaic frescos on the dome of its lobby depict HSBC's offices in eight cities including London, New York, Paris, Tokyo, Hong Kong and Shanghai, all being international financial centers back then. Opinions differ as to why the frescoes were

Shanghai Pudong Development Bank

The Male Villa built in 1936

covered up, but according to the Shanghai Archives, they would have surely been knocked down for their representation of colonial rule. Fortunately, when Shanghai Municipal Government moved in, the people in charge changed their mind and simply covered the frescoes with plaster instead.

Western adventurers to Shanghai also built quite a number of garden estates west of the Huangpu River. Like the buildings on the Bund, these estates also represented a variety of architectural styles from different western countries. Wealthy people in Shanghai lived in such homes.

Shikumen tenement housing is the most typical housing in Shanghai created to accommodate the rapidly growing population, which jumped from over 200,000 in 1843 to 5,460,000 in early 1949. *Shikumen* in Chinese refers to the stone doorframe used in such houses. The layout of such a house resembles the Chinese character " 丰 ", which stands for "harvest".

Most *shikumen* houses were built in the concession areas controlled by such Western powers as Britain and France. Much cheaper than homes, they grew rapidly in number, accounting for 60% of housing in Shanghai during their heyday.

The life in *shikumen* tenement housing

In earlier times one family lived comfortably in a *shikumen* house. However, as time went by seven to eight households were crammed into a single house. In such an environment a special relationship has developed among neighbors, who have to be civil to each other and willing to help, but at the same time stake out a place for themselves.

Shikumen House

In the 1970s and 1980s, three quarters of Shanghai residents lived in *shikumen* houses, sometimes three or four generations sharing a single room. Seeing no privacy at home, young people had to meet their dates somewhere else.

The flood prevention embankment at the Bund became their favorite place to go. So many of them gathered here that the embankment gained another name in due time, the "Lovers' Wall".

Within walking distance from the Lovers' Wall to its west is a road initially known as Garden Lane, later nicknamed the *Da Malu* (a boulevard for big horses), and finally settled into its present name "Nanjing Road" in 1865. The forerunners of the Chinese retail industry—Sincere Department Store, Yong An Department Store, the Da Xin Co. Ltd., and Xin Xin Company—were first opened on Nanjing Road in four buildings completed in the early 20th century.

In 1998 Nanjing Road underwent a transformation whose scale and scope were unprecedented in its 150 years' history. As a result East Nanjing Road was turned into a 1,033-meter pedestrian-only street, where 324 shops are gathered of which some 113 are old reputable ones well-known throughout China.

In 2004, Hualian Commercial Building resumed the name of its predecessor, Yong An Department Store, which opened in 1918. Original looks were restored by removing cement blocks from windows to expose cast iron banisters installed in 1918, a symbol of business open-mindedness as well as respect for traditional business culture.

Nanjing Road

Nanjing Road starts to bustle after 9am. Here daily traffic stands at 800,000 on average and 2,000,000 on holidays. Items sold at the famous Hengdeli Watch & Optical Co. Ltd. reflect changes in Shanghai.

The "Four Major Items" thought to reflect an upscale market refer to watches, radios, bicycles and sewing machines. Although twenty years ago Shanghai boasted major name brands for all the four, an average Shanghai household found it no easy job to purchase any one of them. They had to pinch and scrape in order to raise enough funds.

In recent years housing has taken up a larger and larger portion of household expenditure in Shanghai. People's living conditions have improved. Bugaoli (formerly "Cité Bourgogne") on Shaanxi Road, consisting of *shikumen* houses built in 1930, is a municipal level cultural preservation site undergoing renovation coordinated by the municipal government.

Efforts have been made in the urban redevelopment process since the late 1980s to improve the living conditions of Shanghai residents. Some *shikumen* houses of distinctive styles and rich cultural interest are restored. The majority of *shikumen* houses, rundown and low in residual value, have been gradually phased out by modern buildings. At the same time newly developed properties are now home to former residents in the older parts of town.

Between 1998 and 2002, 15 million square meters of urban area in Shanghai were redeveloped and 80 million square meters of new properties were put onto the market. Together they contributed to 20% of the housing available in the Shanghai market.

There was only one building taller than 100 meters in Shanghai 20 years ago. However, Shanghai today is rejuvenated by over 300 skyscrapers, elevated highways and cloverleaf junctions. Urban infrastructure development in Shanghai experienced three stages: at first the government borrowed from banks to finance projects; then capital was raised through land leasing; right now both public and private funds are leveraged. The dynamic economy and

Shanghai is changing everyday.

market system continuously add momentum to the improvement of the city. In 2005, realized infrastructure investment in Shanghai stood at RMB 88.574 billion Yuan. Such heavy investments help Shanghai grow more and more glamorous as time goes by.

The Lovers' Wall on the Bund was transformed into an observatory deck in 1993, on which 200,000 visitors stand each day to admire the enchanting scenery on both banks of the Huangpu River, and to experience the distinctive flavor of Shanghai.

The Shanghai City History Museum was officially opened in 2000. Every item on display here is part of Shanghai's collective memory.

The first Phoenix car was manufactured in Shanghai in 1959. In the 1970s the brand name was changed into Shanghai, the first domestic car brand in China. So far over one million Shanghai cars have been produced.

Santana cars are the first made-in-Shanghai cars used by average Shanghai families starting from 20 years ago. Over one million of them have rolled off the production line at China's first Sino-foreign car manufacturing joint venture.

The first metro line in Shanghai was put into operation in 1995. So far 123 kilometers of metro line tracks are in use, making it the longest complete system in the country.

The first commercial maglev line in the world was put into use in Shanghai in 2002, its maximum speed approaching 430 kph. Shanghai is once again a trendsetter in the world as well as the country.

The Bund Waibaidu Bridge built in 1907 and Broadway Mansions completed in 1934 were considered fashionable places on the bank of the Suzhou River. The Broadway Mansions complex now goes by the name of

Observatory deck on the Bund

Shanghai Mansions. On both banks of the Suzhou River, many factories built in the same time period have been replaced by residential complexes. However, at 50 Moganshan Road on the southern bank of the river, there is still a stretch of time-worn buildings put up around the 1930s by Xinhe Cotton Mill, which was later renamed Chunming Roving Factory.

The 70-year-old Chunming Roving Factory was transformed into a park for the creative industry. Its 40,000 square meters' old factory floors and warehouses is the only industrial property that remains alongside the Suzhou River after the transformation, where more than 100 artists from a dozen countries have set up their studios.

Treatment of the Suzhou River started in 1988: factories and docks were relocated; household waste water was channelled into waste water treatment plants; effluent traps were installed on the upper and lower reaches of the river within the boundaries of Shanghai. With its beauty regained, the Suzhou River has once again become a venue of recreation for residents.

The People's Square in Shanghai used to be the largest race course in the Far East some 100 years ago. After 1949 the square was a place for people to parade and congregate. With a total area of 140,000 square meters, it could accommodate 1,200,000 people. Renovation of the square started in 1988. After renovation it became Shanghai's cultural center where the past, present and future of Shanghai is showcased. With a view of preserving buildings of historical and cultural interests, the entire Shanghai Concert Hall, built in 1930 and weighing 5,650 tons, was moved 66.4 meters during the renovation to its current site.

In July 2001, a fashionable district south of Huaihai Road two kilometers

The People's Square

away from the People's Square was open to business. It soon became a new landmark for Shanghai. It's called Xintiandi.

One Xintiandi serves as clubhouse for Shui On Group from Hong Kong, the land developer. Built in the early 20th century, this four-story building is a rare specimen in Shanghai that looks Western externally but combines many Chinese features inside. Before renovation it was home to over forty families. When Shui On Group launched their Taipingqiao project, the house was restored according to the original design.

Taipingqiao refers to a 52-hectare block of dwellings near Huaihai Road in Shanghai's Luwan District. In 1996, Shui On Group from Hong Kong was entrusted by the Luwan District Government with the redevelopment of Taipingqiao area. On site were dilapidated *shikumen* houses built in the early 20th century. To demolish or to restore; that was the question.

Also on site was a house in which the First National Congress of the Communist Party of China had been held. As a result, a limit was set on the height of new buildings; no wanted the protected treasures or traditional charm of the area to be overpowered by skyscrapers.

A final decision was made: the 30,000-square-meter *shikumen* houses around the First Communist Party National Congress site would receive a facelift and extensive interior renovation. RMB 1.4 billion Yuan was needed for the project, much higher

The Suzhou River

An aerial view of Xintiandi

than the amount needed to demolish the entire area and build from scratch. After renovation the area was renamed Xintiandi. Surprisingly, merchants scrambled to gain a foothold here. The diner operated by Liuli Gong Fang from Taiwan was the earliest tenant.

Although Xintiandi is exclusively on lease, other properties developed in the Taipingqiao redevelopment project sold well. Ten of the world's Top 500 companies have set up offices at Corporate Avenue. People who came to Shanghai to find a foothold in the exotic setting are comfortable settling close to the diverse world of Xintiandi.

Xintiandi, which means "a brave new world" in Chinese, consists of three Chinese characters: *xin*, which stands for "new"; *tian*, which stands for "heaven"; and *di*, which stands for "earth".

Without heaven there wouldn't be earth; without earth there wouldn't be homes; without homes there wouldn't be people. All causal relationships are submerged in the profuse lightings at Xintiandi. Some people compare Xintiandi to a piece of glazed glass for it deflects light from all over the world. And the light source closest to it comes from the serene house here. Eighty-five years ago, 13 young men gathered beside a lamp at 106 Rue Wantz (now Xingye Road) to form the Communist Party of China. They believed that light through this *shikumen* door would illuminate a brave new world.

The site of the First National Congress of the Communist Party of China

Chapter Twenty-Seven

The Height of Pudong, Shanghai

An old house stands at 160 Lujiazui, Pudong, Shanghai. When wealthy merchant Chen Guichun built it in 1914, Lujiazui by the Huangpu River was still a desolate area. As this compound combining Chinese and Western styles was completed, he could "enjoy the open countryside south of the Yangtze River during the day and hear the waves of the Huangpu River at

The Jinmao Tower seen from the nearby old house

night." This compound was the most luxurious residence in Pudong at that time.

When major development initiatives began in Pudong in 1990, bulldozers stopped short of this old house awaiting a decision: to demolish or not to demolish? After some debate the old house was preserved, but in just 15 years' time waves from the Huangpu River were no longer heard at this house, and the open countryside surrounding it have been transformed: Jinmao Tower, the tallest building in China, has sprung up in its yard. This particular scene best epitomizes development in Pudong.

In 1930 the side of Pudong on the eastern bank of the Huangpu River was lined with docks, factories and warehouses. By contrast, across the river on the Bund there stood all sorts of giant western-styled mansions, where all 27 foreign banks present in Shanghai in 1930 were concentrated. Shanghai at that time had already become a center of international trade and finance, and the largest economic powerhouse in the entire Far East.

Shanghai maintained its leadership in prosperity and economy all the way

The night sceneries at Lujiazui

to the 1980s. At that time, a new economic force suddenly rose in the Pearl River Delta and the coastal areas in southern China, posing a great challenge to Shanghai. In 1990, Pudong development initiatives were officially launched. Ever since then developers and builders have been working wonders on the former farmland of Pudong.

On November 19th, 1991, Nanpu Bridge, which linked both banks of the Huangpu River, was open to traffic.

On July 30th, 1991, the first pile of a 468-meter tower was driven into the ground at Lujiazui. This television tower was named Oriental Pearl. In over a year's time the tower rose to 360 meters.

Its designers were imaginative enough to arrange eleven spheres, or "pearls", of different sizes up to a height of 350 meters. At a total height of 468 meters, the Oriental Pearl Tower is the highest in Asia.

In July 1994, right before the completion of the Oriental Pearl Tower, *Architecture Today* in the U.K. ran a cover story entitled *The Height of Shanghai*, in which it wrote, "The huge size and multi-spherical shape of the Shanghai TV Tower makes it a symbol of Shanghai, like what the Eiffel Tower is to Paris and the London Bridge to London."

Since its opening on November 18th, 1994, the Oriental Pearl Tower has been receiving an average of several thousand tourists who can access the three larger pearls, the lowest and the largest of which, perching 90 meters above ground with a circular corridor 50 meters in diameter, houses the

Shanghai seen from the 39th floor of the Jinmao Tower

transmitters on the upper deck and a sightseeing area on the lower deck.

The Oriental Pearl Tower is located right on the tip of Lujiazui. Across the river from it is the bustling Nanjing Road. Yangpu Bridge and Nanpu Bridge flank it like "two dragons playing with a pearl". Thanks to the Oriental Pearl, people can appreciate the Huangpu River, the mother river of Shanghai, from a newer and higher position.

In a conference room at the Lujiazui Finance and Trade Zone Development Co. Ltd., one can still find the models prepared over ten years ago by famous design houses from Britain, France, Japan, Italy and China when they competed to win the bid to plan the 28-square-kilometer area of Lujiazui. At that time, construction of the Oriental Pearl Tower had already started. In October 1992, a panel of more than 30 experts from around the world awarded the contract to the Shanghai joint design team, requesting that the latter integrate commendable features from competitive designs into their own.

Right before the Oriental Pearl Tower was open to public, another landmark sprung up at Lujiazui, the 88-story 420.5-meter Jinmao Tower, the highest in Pudong as well as China.

On August 28 1997 the roof of Jinmao Tower was sealed. A location-hunting German arrived at the building although fittings were still going on. On that day Joachim Maedler simply looked out of a 39th-floor window and decided this was it. Although he was not sure what the building would eventually look like, the view outside was enough to convince him.

The 33-storey atrium inside Grand Hyatt Shanghai at Jinmao Tower resembles a time tunnel. In four months' time Joachim Maedler moved into the 39th floor of the building with his entire staff at Dresden Bank A.G.'s Shanghai office. One look out of the window and his bank became the first business to set up quarters at the tallest building in Pudong.

On the Bund across the Huangpu River there used to be a German bank more than 80 years ago, a Deutsche Asiastische Bank, of which Dresden Bank was a shareholder. Following Dresden, 157 businesses moved into the office area of Jinmao Tower.

In less than ten years' time all major banks relocated to the Lujiazui Finance and Trade Zone along with more than 230 of the top 500 companies in the world, making Pudong the new financial center of the city. Following their lead, at least sixty four multinational companies have moved their headquarters from around the world to the riverside of Pudong.

On October 5th, 2003, 15 parachutists from different countries leapt into the air from the top of Jinmao Tower, an act far more significant than a mere stunt. To land in Lujiazui is to share the rapid growth of the Chinese economy.

A highly modernized Lujiazui accommodates the old house at the foot of Jinmao Tower; and the old house keeps a record of all important milestones in Pudong's development over the past ten-odd years. The old house is now Lujiazui Development Museum.

This old house is the only one to have survived redevelopment. Ten years ago it was one of the many dwellings where over 3,500 families lived. Right now it is well blended into a 100,000-square-meter green space surrounded by beautiful giants.

When famous British architect Richard Rogers saw the planning for Lujiazui development done by the Shanghai joint design team in 1992, he was amazed by the Chinese ability of understanding and integrating design styles from different countries. However, what is even more amazing to the world is the Chinese ability and speed in turning such drawings into reality.

On November 18th, 1984, the first stock in China was issued in Shanghai.

Two major events took place in Shanghai in 1990, both leaving positive impact on the city: the launching of major development initiatives in Pudong; and the establishment of Shanghai Stock Exchange on December 19th. The ballroom at Astor House Hotel with a glass sunshade once reputed to be the biggest in the Far East was turned into the trading floor of the Shanghai Stock Exchange.

Over the last dozen years, the non-permanent population in Pudong has increased by over 1.2 million. Coming from all corners of the earth, they smile with the same optimistic confidence as the earlier settlers in Shanghai. Many expatriates have brought their families to Pudong and adopted Chinese names. They are all warmly referred to as Pudongese.

A legion of multinational companies has injected new life into Pudong. Pharmaceutical giants in the world tried to forestall each other by setting up facilities at the Zhangjiang Hi-Tech Park, their investment per hectare exceeding US$18 million. Using development experience in the Pearl River Delta for reference, Zhangjiang Hi-Tech Park has managed to attract 60 projects with a total investment of more than US$ 1.2 billion, almost all of which are knowledge-based industries.

Night view of Nanpu Bridge

In 2005, the Port of Shanghai, strategically located at the estuary of the 6,380-kilometer Yangtze River, became the world's largest freight port with annual traffic of 443 million tons, quite an achievement for a port known only by its historic reputation until recently.

At sunset each day, the Oriental Pearl is the first on both banks of the Huangpu River to light up. Without major development initiatives launched in 1990, a dimly lit eastern bank could hardly compete with the resplendent western bank. As the clock at the Customs House chimes on, Pudong becomes an ever bright spot on the nightscape.

When major development initiatives were first launched in 1990, there wasn't a single bridge spanning the Huangpu River, which divides Shanghai into Pudong and Puxi (meaning "East of Huangpu River" and "West of Huangpu River" respectively). The only means of transportation available were ferryboats. Pudong and Puxi was linked the first time in history by the completion of Nanpu Bridge on November 19th, 1991, under which 50,000-ton vessels can still sail.

In September 1993 Yangpu Bridge was completed. Again a cable stayed bridge, its surface just two meters taller above the river than Nanpu Bridge.

A mere half year later, construction on a third cable stayed bridge spanning the Huangpu River began on April 1st, 1994. The Xupu Bridge was open to

The "Oriental Light" sundial

traffic in only three years' time.

When a decision was made to build a fourth bridge on the Huangpu River, the designer-in-chief of all four bridges started to consider whether it was a good idea to build yet another cable stayed bridge.

On December 13th, 2002, when Lupu Bridge, the longest steel arch bridge in the world, was still under construction, Shanghai won the bid to host the 2010 World Expo. The 5.28-square-kilometer area between Nanpu Bridge and Lupu Bridge on both banks of the Huangpu River was chosen to be the site for the World Expo.

Over 200,000 square meters' industrial property, including Jiangnan Shipyard, China's largest shipyard, will be transformed into the pavilions for various countries.

According to planning the former slipway at Jiangnan Shipyard will be transformed into a large outdoor sunken stage by 2010. During the 185 days in which the World Expo takes place, it will be the center stage of the world on which more than 1,000 shows will be performed.

Pudong with its total area of 520 square kilometers is the largest urban development zone in China. Someone compared its takeoff to "an epoch-making takeoff from the ridge of a field."

On the evening of October 20th, 2001, a firework display in honor of the APEC Shanghai meeting lit up both sides of the Huangpu River as well as the sky of this metropolitan city.

Together with Jinmao Tower, a huge sundial named the Oriental Light won a gold prize for architecture upon the tenth anniversary of the opening up of Pudong. A sundial is an ancient Chinese chronograph.

The needle of the sundial points to the distant outer space, where Shenzhou V, China's first manned spacecraft, once took pictures of the Yangtze River Delta at night. The brightest spots on those images include the Yangtze River estuary, Pudong, Shanghai and even the entire Yangtze River. A new round of major transformation is on its way.

Chapter Twenty-Eight
Where the Yangtze Empties into the Sea

Chongming Island is the world's largest estuary alluvial island.

Over 2,000 years ago the Yangtze River joined the sea at today's Jiangyin County of Jiangsu Province. As more sand carried by the river was deposited, both the northern and the southern banks of the estuary expanded, and the shoals in the midst of the river gradually evolved into the Chongming, Changxing and Hengsha Islands. Chongming Island divides the Yangtze River estuary into two parts. The northern course is as narrow as 2.4 kilometers at its narrowest; whereas the southern course, with a minimum breadth of 8.3 kilometers and a maximum of 60 kilometers, is regarded as the main course of the river.

For years it has been boats that link Chongming Island with either bank of the Yangtze River. In recent years modern high-speed boats facilitate the flow of people and materials between Chongming Island and the outside world. Right now there are 700,000 registered residents on the island, of whom, close to 50,000 make their living elsewhere. Meanwhile over 60,000 people have arrived from other parts of the country to live and work on the island. Thanks to sand deposition by the Yangtze River Chongming Island grows at an annual speed of approximately 20,000 mu. At present with a total area of 1,411 square kilometers it is the third largest island in China.

Chongming is a county under the jurisdiction of the Shanghai Municipal

The satellite remote sensing map of the estuary of the Yangtze River

Dongtan Wetland

Government. The county seat is located at Chenqiao, a town of 100,000 people. The pedestrian-only street here in town may not be as bustling as Nanjing Road, but local residents and visitors alike could still enjoy the lively but leisurely atmosphere accompanied by sea breezes and pop music.

Chongming islanders today are mostly offspring of early settlers who arrived at the island since the days of the Song Dynasty from Changshu, Jurong and other places in Jiangsu Province to fish, make salt, and set up wasteland.

Chongming Island is still young. The first two shoals—Dongsha and Xisha—emerged in the Tang Dynasty. Yaoliusha came into being in the North Song Dynasty. Starting from the Yuan Dynasty the increasing number of shoals joined to form an island. By late Ming Dynasty and early Qing Dynasty Chongming was already a big island 100 kilometers in length and 20 kilometers in width.

It took more than 1,300 years' work by the Yangtze River and the sea to create the Chongming Island of today. When Zhu Yuanzhang, the First Emperor of the Ming Dynasty, called Chongming Island a "Fairy Land on East China Sea", agriculture started to develop into a mainstay of the island economy as soil salinity dropped. Major land reclamation from marshes on the island began in 1959. After the founding of the People's Republic of China, the Shanghai Municipal Government mobilized 100,000 people to reclaim land from marshes on Chongming Island and other seaside areas in order to feed the exploding population.

In early reclamation projects people carried mud with shoulder poles. The many dykes on the island mark their tremendous efforts.

Between 1956 and 1984 around 612,569 *mu* of land was reclaimed, more than one third of the island's total area. Chongming Island became the storage barn for Shanghai's growing food needs.

Changxing Island of Shanghai

Natural evolution on Chongming Island has not been disrupted by continuous reclamation efforts. Shoals formed by sedimentation are soon overgrown with such wild plants as reeds and a renewable chain of life is formed. Scientists call such a landform "wetland". Dongtan, an area over 200 kilometers on the eastern tip of Chongming Island, is the only coastal wetland undamaged by human intervention and remains a haven to hundreds of birds, wild flora and fauna.

In July 2005 the jurisdiction over the other two islands of the Yangtze River estuary—Hengsha Island and Changxing Island—was turned over to Chongming County, triggering synergized development among the three islands. Hengsha Island, the smallest of the three, will develop into an eco-tourism destination with forest covering 70% of the land.

Changxing Island, the closest of the three to downtown Shanghai and Wusongkou, will become the only manufacturing base for offshore equipment. On it Shanghai Zhenhua Port Machinery Co. Ltd. has set up a world-class manufacturing base whose products dominate 50% of the global market. Next to it a shipbuilding base belonging to China State Shipbuilding Corporation is under construction. The 140-year-old Jiangnan Shipyard has relocated here from the bank of Huangpu River is to develop into "New Jiangnan", a top-notch shipbuilding facility in the world with a capacity of three million metric tons.

The tunnel-and-bridge project launched in 2004 will connect Pudong and

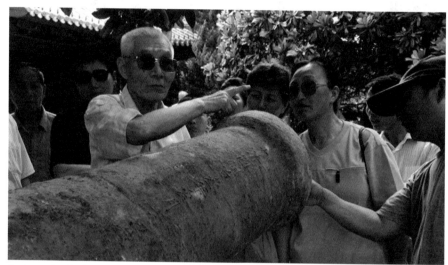

Baoshan ancient Emplacement

Changxing Island with a tunnel beneath the southern course of the Yangtze River, Changxing Island and Chongming Island with a bridge, and Qidong, Haimen in Jiangsu Province and Chongming Island with another bridge over the northern course of the Yangtze River. When the project is completed, the three Yangtze River estuary islands will be linked to both banks of the Yangtze River.

Wusongkou at Baoshan District is the gateway to the Yangtze and Huangpu Rivers. Iron cannons excavated in recent years are evidence to resistance efforts against foreign invasion at Wusongkou in history.

Located on the land strip formed by the Yangtze River and Huangpu River more than 1,400 years ago, Baoshan District covers an area of about 300 square kilometers. Upon completion of a river tunnel in 2003, Baoshan was further integrated into the rest of Shanghai, including Pudong, via the Outer Ring Road of Shanghai. As an important shipping base in Shanghai, Baoshan boasts twenty-two 10,000-ton-and-above docks handling over 10 million containers with an annual import and export traffic of more than 23 million tons.

Baoshan (meaning "Precious Hill" in Chinese) got its name from Yangtze River transportation: an artificial hill was erected at Wusongkou during the

The confluence point of the Huangpu River and the Yangtze River

reign of Emperor Yongle, who named it "Precious Hill", to guide inbound and outbound ships at Wusongkou.

The last tributary to join the Yangtze River before it empties into the sea, Huangpu River meets the Yangtze River at Wusongkou, which is 27 kilometers from the Bund bordering on Baoshan in the west, Pudong in the east, and the Yangtze River in the north.

The artificial hill has already been washed out by tidewater. The ban on maritime trade imposed in early Qing Dynasty drove ships away from the broad river here. Wusongkou revived when Shanghai was opened to foreign trade more than 160 years ago. Day and night vessels come in or go out, projecting Shanghai into a trajectory of prosperity. Wusongkou has once again become China's gateway into global economy.

Navigation Mark 101 at Wusongkou demarcates Huangpu River from the Yangtze River. The water route here has been the busiest in China for more than 100 years. Across from Navigation Mark 101 is a lighthouse built by the Dutch some 100 years ago to mark the confluence of the Yangtze River and Huangpu River.

The headstream of Huangpu River was identified in 1999 when experts from the Shanghai Geographical Association traced the river all the way back to Longwang Hill in northern Tianmu Mountain, where they put finger on a stream of spring water, known to locals as Xitiao Stream, which drops from a hilltop more than 1,500 meters above sea level.

When Xitiao Stream joins Dongtiao Stream, another tributary of Huangpu River, before arriving at Huzhou, it is already large enough to float a boat. Afterwards it flows into the Tai Lake and then the Dianshan Lake to reach Shanghai.

Huangpu River traverses Shanghai before joining the Yangtze River, leaving behind it Pudong and Puxi, both comparable to children of Huangpu River and yet 100 years apart from each other in age.

On November 17th, 1978, the first pile of Shanghai Baosteel was driven into the bank of the Yangtze River. This steel complex, which went on to become the largest in China, covers an area of 22 square kilometers on the land strip between the Yangtze River and Huangpu River. The location at the Yangtze River estuary was ideal for Baosteel, a large importer of complete sets of advanced equipment as well as high quality iron ore that needs dedicated oceangoing vessels.

Right now Baosteel boasts two 12-meter-deep raw material docks where freight ships below 100,000 tons can moor and unload. A 52-kilometer conveyor belt sends iron ore directly from docks to workshops. It took 23 years and three phases to finish the construction of Baosteel in 2001. In 1998, Baosteel evolved into China's largest steel conglomerate—Shanghai Baosteel Group. At present the group, with its annual steelmaking capacity of 20 million tons, comes out on top of all global steelmakers and is listed as one of the top 500 steel producers in the world.

It takes 56 million tons of water for Baosteel to produce 14 million tons of steel every year. Thanks to advanced water recycling technology, Baosteel fetches a mere 200,000 tons of water from the Yangtze River every year and discharges no waste water at all. Science, technology and management contribute to Baosteel's advanced water utilization system. At Baosteel there is neither fume nor foul smell. Instead lawns and trees thrive alongside office buildings, furnaces and workshops.

In spring and autumn each year, more than two million migratory birds

Shoals of the Chongming Island

that travel between Australia and Siberia sojourn at Dongtan Wetland on Chongming Island to renew their strength to finish the 7,000-kilometer journey. Among the close to 100 types of migratory birds there are quite a number on the verge of extinction. Dongtan has become the largest migratory bird preserve in East Asia.

An underdeveloped pocket of land at the Yangtze River estuary, Chongming Island is an "Everlasting Oasis" for the Yangtze River. It holds great ecological potential for the future growth of Shanghai.

Today, at the Yangtze River estuary, shoals are still expanding into the sea, and the natural wonder of turning ocean into land is still going on. The oasis at the estuary will extend too.

Here the Yangtze River, our mother river, finally finds its home. Here is the end to a glistening silver ribbon on earth.

In 2006, the floating light at the Yangtze River estuary marking the confluence point of the Yangtze River with the East China Sea is located at East Latitude 122°28'09", some 8.5 kilometers to the east of the confluence point twenty years before.

The crabs on the Dongtan Wetland

Afterword

Map of the Yangtze River water system

Rising from the Jianggendiru glacier at the snow-draped Gela Dandong on the Qinghai-Tibet Plateau, the Yangtze River, together with scores of major tributaries, traverses China in its 6380-kilometer meter course that drops over 5,400 meters on its way. It is a mother river to the great Chinese nation.

Viewed from above, the water system at the source of the Yangtze River resembles braids tossed into the air or blood vessels, pumping with life. At the estuary water currents leave traces on newly formed land. Both ends of the Yangtze River are so alike that they testify the resilient power of life they carry.

Two million years ago human beings appeared in the Yangtze River Basin. Ever since then generations of people have depended on the great river for their living. The Yangtze River is an invaluable gift from nature to people. Year in, year out, from land to grains, it brings people everything they need.

It is a great river belonging to all kinds of life, from bird to beast, from flora to fauna. For hundreds of billions of years nature has ruled the earth in its own way, dictating evolution or elimination. Until now human beings find it impossible to predict the consequence of undue extinction of species. It is unknown what will result from lost lives in the Yangtze River. It falls on our shoulders to protect the Yangtze River.

Pupils from Tuotuo River Primary School, the first school in the Yangtze

Pupils at the source of the Yangtze River

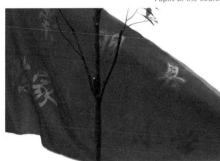

Pupils at the estuary of the Yangtze River

River source area, are having their weekly after-school program. In comparison to their peers elsewhere, the pupils here are more mature and more aware of their responsibility. Right under their feet is the virgin land of the Yangtze River source area.

Every spring, pupils from the Chenjia Town Central Primary School on Chongming Island will plant trees on land near the sea. Pupils from the last primary school along the Yangtze River course are adding one final touch of green to the river before it joins the sea.

This is a common scene on the banks of the Yangtze River. This joy is exclusive to people living on river banks, blessed by the Yangtze River.

A complete map of the Yangtze River water system resembles the main and collateral channels for blood and qi in a human body. Water is like the blood, or the qi. The main and collateral channels for blood and Chi in a human body make perception and emotions possible. Likewise, the Yangtze River is also alive. To care for life with life, this is the new perception and emotion of the Chinese nation towards their mother river.

It is filled with people's best wishes and prayers as the river water rushes thousands of miles towards the sea, where yet another cycle of life begins.